PIONEER STORIES

Children all over the world who look for and love the coming of Jesus.

PIONEER STORIES OF THE SECOND ADVENT MESSAGE

by
Arthur Whitefield Spalding

TEACH Services, Inc.
PUBLISHING
www.TEACHServices.com

World rights reserved. This book or any portion thereof may not be copied or reproduced in any form or manner whatever, except as provided by law, without the written permission of the publisher, except by a reviewer who may quote brief passages in a review.

This book was written to provide truthful information in regard to the subject matter covered. The author assumes full responsibility for the accuracy of all facts and quotations as cited in this book. The opinions expressed in this book are the author's personal views and interpretation of the Bible, Spirit of Prophecy, and/or contemporary authors and do not necessarily reflect those of TEACH Services, Inc.

This book is sold with the understanding that the publisher is not engaged in giving spiritual, legal, medical, or other professional advice. If authoritative advice is needed, the reader should seek the counsel of a competent professional.

This book played a formative role in the development of Christian thought and the publisher feels that this book, with its candor and depth, still holds significance for the church today. It has been reformatted and the original page numbers have been included where each page ends, indicated by a page number in square brackets, e.g. "[iii]," "[10]". Because of this reformatting some of the illustrations may not fall in their original location.

Copyright © 1995, 2012 TEACH Services, Inc.
ISBN-13: 978-1-57258-042-8 (Paperback)
ISBN-13: 978-1-57258-983-4 (ePub)
ISBN-13: 978-1-57258-790-8 (Kindle/Mobi)
Library of Congress Control Number: 95061167

Published by

www.TEACHServices.com

DEDICATION

This book is dedicated to
CHILDREN ALL OVER THE WORLD
who look for and love
THE COMING OF JESUS
and especially to the
CHILDREN OF THE BETHEL CHURCH SCHOOL
whose daily request for "another true story" were
a constant inspiration to the
writing of these

FOREWORD

It is good for children to know what their fathers and mothers did; for sometimes that makes a pattern of what the children should do. Especially is this true if the children are set to finish the work their parents began. And that is the reason why this book is written, to tell the children of the pioneers in the Second Advent movement the beginnings of that movement, and the reasons why they are to carry on.

When this advent message began, the signs of the break-up of the world were few, but in our day they have multiplied a thousand times. The promise of Jesus that He would come again has ever been a beacon of hope to His followers; and the darker the world the brighter the light. They who love the Lord will eagerly look for every sign that He is coming soon. Those signs are clustering fast; we have not long to wait.

The feet of the pioneers trod a rough and heavy road. They have passed away, and their [11] tasks have become ours. Today it is the privilege not only of grown people but of children also to finish the work, to complete the journey to the City of God. May these stories of the pioneers in this great advent movement inspire many a child and youth to carry on where their fathers led the way, and soon bring the kingdom of Jesus.

ARTHUR W. SPALDING
Madison College, Tennessee, 1942 [12]

CONTENTS

Part One

I	Coming Again	11
II	Preparing a Messenger	17
III	The Message Begins	26
IV	The Message Spreads	33
V	In the West	38
VI	In the South	46
VII	In the North	54
VIII	Herald to England	60
IX	Missionary to the World	50
X	Children in Sweden	77
XI	Children in America	83
XII	The Midnight Cry	93
XIII	The Disappointment	101

Part Two

XIV	Light on the Sanctuary	110
XV	The Sabbath	118
XVI	The Spirit of Prophecy	124
XVII	The Opening Heavens and the Unchanged Law	129
XVIII	Two New Workers	135
XIX	Printing the Truth	140
XX	Moving to Michigan	144
XXI	Preaching in Poverty	148
XXII	The Health Work	154
XXIII	Camp Meeting	161
XXIV	The First Foreign Mission	166
XXV	Selling the Books	172
XXVI	Visiting an African Chief	176
XXVII	The Pitcairn	181
XXVIII	What You Were Born For	188

PART ONE

A little company of young men gathered around their Teacher on a high hill.

I

COMING AGAIN

One day, very long ago, a little company of young men gathered around their Teacher on a high hill that looked over the great city of Jerusalem. The hill was called the Mount of Olives, because a great many olive trees grew on its sides. It was a beautiful place then, with thick-leaved trees and grassy slopes and flowers sprinkled everywhere; for this was in the springtime, and everything was fresh and green.

And the men sat there and looked down on the city, with its dazzling white-and-gold temple, and thought how beautiful it was. But they were very sad; for they had just heard that that strong and glorious temple should sometime be thrown down and utterly destroyed. They knew the temple had been made for God, and He was worshiped there every day; and they thought it surely never could be thrown down until the end of the world, when everything would be destroyed.

It was Jesus, their Teacher, who had told them it would be destroyed; and now four of them, whose names were Peter and Andrew and [17] James and John, came close to Him, to ask Him more about it. Jesus was sitting on the hill, looking, oh, so sad, as He gazed down upon the temple and the city; for He knew that the people would have to suffer awful things, and He was sorry for them, sorrier than you or I could be. The men came softly up and sat down around Him, and they said: "Tell us, when shall these [18] things be? And what shall be the sign of Thy coming, and of the end of the world?"

They had just heard that the strong and glorious temple should sometime be thrown down.

Now Jesus knew that the world would not come to an end when Jerusalem and the temple should be destroyed. But He knew that these men, His disciples, could not understand if He should tell them all that would happen before the end of the world, and so He did not try. But He thought, "The poor people will have to suffer so much when Jerusalem is destroyed, that it will be a great deal like the end of the world, and I will tell them about both those times together." And so He told them the story of what was going to come. You can read it in the very words He used in the twenty-fourth chapter of Matthew, but I am to tell the story very much as Jesus might have told it to you.

"Be careful," He said, "not to let any one deceive you. There will be many men who say they are Christ, and a great many people will believe them, and do what they tell them to. But if you hear that Christ is over in Bethel, or over in Jericho, or somewhere else, or out in the country, or hiding Himself in some house, don't believe it. Do you want to know how you can tell when I really come again? Well, you remember how some dark night you [19] have seen the lightning flash? Though it was away ever so far, you could see it, and its light would be seen from the east away to the west. Just as clearly as that will everybody see Me when I come again, with all the holy angels.

"You will hear of many wars," He went on, "but don't be troubled; for before the end comes, many nations will have terrible wars, and there will be famines and earthquakes in different places. But these are only small troubles; for you will be hated by everybody because you love Me. Even some whom you have loved will hate you, and give you up to be killed. But whoever will endure to the end, he shall be saved. And the good news of My coming again shall be told in all the world, so that all nations will hear of it, and then shall the end come."

The men were listening very closely to what Jesus was telling them; and now, when He told them that the "gospel" or the "good news" must be carried everywhere to all the world before He should come again, they could see something they had to do in bringing the end. And there is just the same thing now for every one to do who loves Jesus and wants Him to come.

Then He told them the signs He would give after these things, so that they might know His coming was near. I am going to give you the [20] exact words He said, and it is well for you to learn them, for they are famous words of prophecy: "Immediately after the tribulation of those days shall the sun be darkened, and the moon shall not give her light, and the stars shall fall from heaven, and the powers of the heavens shall be shaken: and then shall appear the sign of the Son of man in heaven: and then shall all the tribes of the earth mourn, and they shall see the Son of man coming in the clouds of heaven with power and great glory. And He shall send His angels with a great sound of a trumpet, and they shall gather together His elect from the four winds, from one end of heaven to the other."

Down the hill a little way was a fig tree growing. It was yet early spring, and the trees were putting out their leaves. The fig tree had brought out its small green figs, and now the leaves were beginning to show.

Pioneer Stories

And Jesus said, "Learn a lesson from the fig tree, and all the trees. When it puts out its leaves, you know that summer is near. Just so, when you see all these signs I have told you of, know that the end is very near."

Jesus' disciples sat there listening and thinking. Some of them sat gazing into His face, while some of them were looking down upon the city and the temple. And they all were very [21] quiet, for what Jesus had told them seemed very wonderful and very awful. You can see Peter's face, dark and troubled; and John's, full of eagerness as he watches his Teacher's eyes. They all thought the future seemed very dark. But Jesus was good to them in not telling them all the terrible things He knew were really coming; for they could not have endured hearing them.

Down the hill a little way was a fig tree growing.

Away beyond the city, in the west, the sun was going down, and the night was drawing near. Just so, it seemed to the disciples, Jesus had been bringing to their minds a night that was coming on all the world; for the things He had been telling were very dark. And so they were; and the hundreds of years in which the things happened [22] that He told of, men still call the "Dark Ages." We are hardly out of that night yet, but we are very near the morning, as you shall find out soon. Jesus' coming will be the breaking of the day.

The next few days after Jesus told this story to His disciples were the most wonderful and the most terrible and the most glorious days that have ever been on this earth. For in those days was settled the fate of this world and of you and me and of every other person living or who has ever lived. In those days Jesus, the Son of God, gave up His life to save the world, and that was the most wonderful thing ever known. And in those days wicked men, driven by the devil, crucified the Son of God, and that was the most terrible of all the terrible things that have ever been. And in those days, through the sacrifice of Jesus, good triumphed over evil, life triumphed over death, God triumphed over Satan; and that was the most glorious thing that ever was. For though Jesus entered into death, God raised Him again the third day, to live forevermore, and to give life eternal to those who follow Him.

Some forty days afterward, Jesus led His disciples again to the Mount of Olives. And He said to them: "You are to give to the whole world the good news of salvation through My death and life. Begin at Jerusalem, and go out [23] to the utmost parts of the earth." Then He lifted up His hands and blessed them. And as He blessed them, He was taken from them up into the air, and a shining cloud of angels received Him. While the disciples stood gazing steadily after Him, and wondering if He had left them indeed, Jesus sent back two angels to give them again His message. The angels, clad all in white, stood by the disciples, and said: "Men of Galilee, why do you stand gazing up into heaven? This same Jesus, who is taken up from you into heaven, shall come again, come in like manner as you have seen Him go into heaven."

That is the sure promise of Jesus. He is coming again. The signs that He gave to show His coming near have most of them been fulfilled. It is now the time of the end of the world and of the second advent of Jesus. God's great clock of time keeps longer hours than those we have. A little day sometimes seems long to us, a little year may seem an age; but to God a thousand years are but as a day. So, though the time of the end is here, and the time when Jesus shall appear in His glory, it may not be at just the time when we expect it. But it will come, and in God's thought it will come soon.

Over a hundred years ago men were moved by God to start the message of Jesus' soon [24] coming. A hundred years is more than you have lived, it is more than I have lived, it is more than almost any person now lives. And still, after a hundred years, the work is not finished, and Jesus has not come. Yet He is coming; for He has promised; and a hundred years in His sight may be but as a moment. Day by day and year by year the signs show ever more clearly that His coming is very near. Now I shall tell you stories of the men and the women who were pioneers in this great message of Jesus' coming again, pioneers of the second advent message. [25]

II

PREPARING A MESSENGER

The man whom God used to start the Second Advent message in America was William Miller. He was born during the American Revolution, in 1782. His father and mother then lived on a farm in the western hills of Massachusetts, but when little William was four years old, they moved into New York, to a place called Low Hampton, which is a few miles from the south end of Lake Champlain. Can you find this long lake on the map? It lies between New York and Vermont. It was new country then, and the father of little William Miller, whose name was also William Miller, built a log cabin for his family, and set to work to clear a farm for himself. So William Miller grew up to be a big boy, sturdy, broad-shouldered, and square-faced. As soon as be was big enough, he took hold of the work with his father in the clearing and on the farm; for he was the oldest of sixteen brothers and sisters, and you can imagine the father needed all the help that his son could give him.

He found very little time for school; and, anyway, nobody in that place then could get [26] more than three months of schooling a year; for that was all the time the school held. But his mother taught him to read, and be devoured all the few books there were in the house, so that when he did go to school, he went into the class with the big boys and girls. He loved to read, and he used to sit by the fireplace nights, with a blazing pine knot for light, and read until after all the other people were in bed. The Bible, the psalmbook, and the prayer book formed his chief reading until be was ten years of age.

He used to read till after all the other people were in bed.

Sitting in the chimney corner when a party was gathered at his father's house, he would listen to the men telling stories of the War for Independence, and be longed to have books that would tell him more. So one of the first he got after this was a history of the United States. [27] You know our nation was not very old then, and the histories were made up of stories of Washington and Franklin and others, more than of mere facts and dates, like ours today. He was very proud of his country, and he made up his mind he would always stand for the liberties these men had won if he should find them in danger.

When William had grown up to be a young man, he wished very much to go to college, but his father wanted him to stay on the farm. He had already learned all he could at the school there, and he wished to become a learned man. He tried and tried to plan some way to go, but all his plans came to nothing. Yet God trained him better, perhaps, than He could have trained him in college, for the work He wanted him to do.

William Miller married in 1803, and with his wife moved to a farm at Poultney, Vt., a few miles southeast of Low Hampton. He grew to be very popular with the people here, and came to be a man of influence. The young people used to flock to his house for parties, and everybody wanted him and his wife whenever there was going to be "a good time."

But the sad part of it is, he grew away from God. The men he associated with were the great men of the place, the thinkers and doers, but [29] most of them did not believe in Jesus. William Miller began to read the books they

Preparing a Messenger

read, and he came, like his companions, not to believe in Christ or in the Bible. They believed there was a God, but that He had not much to do with men, and they did not think that Jesus had died to save them from their sins, or that there would be any judgment day. They believed that when they died, that would be the end of it, and they would never live again. Such people are called deists, and for years William Miller was a deist.

He was a soldier for two years, in the War of 1812, and some things he went through at that time made him think very seriously about the Christian religion. Still he did not give up his unbelief, but after the war returned to his farm still a deist. At this time he moved back to Low Hampton, where his mother was still living, though his father was dead.

His father had run into debt, and put a mortgage on his farm to get some money. William Miller paid off the mortgage, and gave the farm to his mother and his brother Solomon, so his mother lived there near him until her death. He bought another farm for himself, half a mile away.

There, on a little hill, he built a comfortable two-story farm house, and planted around it the rose and lilac bushes so dear to the New England heart. From the east room, which was his library and study, he could see two miles away to the Poultney River and the little village of Fairhaven. On the other side of the house, a few rods away, was a beautiful grove, of which we shall hear more afterwards. By this grove the road led to the big town of Whitehall, eight miles to the west, where the lake boats from the north unloaded their freight upon the canal boats that took it down to the Hudson River and to New York City.

Miller's grandfather, his mother's father, was a good old Baptist minister, and he sometimes came to Low Hampton to preach. After awhile there came to be a company of Baptists in that place, and there was built near William Miller's farmhouse a little church, or chapel, for them to meet in. Miller, though he was not a Christian, used to go to this chapel on Sunday, to please his mother. He liked well enough, for that matter, to hear the ministers preach; but sometimes there were no ministers to preach, and then one of the deacons would read from the book of sermons. When they were to read, William Miller would stay away; and when his mother asked him why, he said the deacons couldn't read well enough. Then one of the deacons, [30] hearing of this, came to Miller and asked him to do the reading. I suppose he felt rather ashamed to have this good man heap coals of fire on his head like that; but he said he would read. And after that, when there was no minister to preach, William Miller would read the sermons he didn't believe to the people who did believe them.

There was built near William Miller's farmhouse a little church.

His grandfather and other ministers, who came sometimes to big meetings at Low Hampton, used to stay at his house, and though he liked to argue with them and try to show that they were foolish to believe in Jesus, he was glad to have them stay with him and his family, and they always had a pleasant visit there. [31]

But the time was near when he was to be changed. He was not what we would call a wicked man. He was not a drunkard, nor cruel, nor profane; he was honest with everybody, and always kind to big people and little people. Everybody thought him as good as anybody else, and better than a good many; and I suppose he thought so himself. But did you ever hear what a wise man once said: "The heart is deceitful above all things, and desperately wicked?" He did not know how wicked he really was, just as we do not know how wicked we really are.

But one day he caught himself swearing. It shocked him, and he went off by himself to the beautiful grove west of his house, and started thinking. He began to wonder whether there really might be a life after this life on earth.

Preparing a Messenger

The more he thought, the less he could tell; but of one thing he was sure, that if after his death he should never live again, that was very terrible; and if, on the other hand, he should live again, at the judgment day, and have to be judged righteous or guilty for what he had done, he would be found guilty, and that would be more terrible still. So it went on for some months, and he was very unhappy. He was now thirty-four years old. [32]

The people of his neighborhood were going to have a big celebration that year, in memory of a battle the Americans had won in the War of 1812. William Miller had been in that battle, and his neighbors all decided on him as the one to take charge of the celebration. They were going to have a ball,—that is, a dance,—and Captain Miller had a number of young men as his staff of helpers to make the preparations. These young men were gathered at the Miller house the day before, when someone proposed that they all should go to hear a minister who was to preach that evening. So in the evening the whole company started off, laughing and talking, and [33] having great fun over the thought of how they were going to celebrate the next night. They weren't thinking at all of a good religious meeting, but were going just to pass the time.

Mrs. Miller stayed at home. Along late in the evening she heard the young

The whole company started off, laughing and talking.

men come tramping back, but they were not laughing now, nor talking, nor singing songs. They were very quiet when they came in. She asked them many questions about the meeting and the sermon, but they didn't seem to want to talk. Then she tried asking them about what they were going to do to get ready for the ball next night, but they didn't want to talk about that either. So she came to the conclusion that they had been pretty well sobered by what they had heard at the church. Afterwards her husband told her that the minister had spoken from a text that said: "Run! Speak to this young man," and he talked so straight to the people about their sins and their need of repentance that every young man there thought the minister surely meant just him. They didn't feel like having their ball next night, and so it was put off, and they never had it.

The next Sunday, Miller was to read the sermon at the church. He started to read, but he felt so bad he couldn't control his voice, and [34] he stopped and sat down. They all felt very sorry for him. He went home from that meeting very wretched. He felt that he was very bad, and that he couldn't make himself good. And he knew that he ought to be punished for his sins, but the only punishment as great as his sins would be death, and he wanted to live. Then suddenly the thought came to him, If there were somebody so good, who had never sinned, who would be willing to take his place and the place of all who had sinned, and die for them, oh, how wonderful and loving such a person would be. Then he thought, That was just what Jesus was said to have done. But only the Bible told of Jesus, and if he didn't believe the Bible, how could he be saved from his crushing load of sins? So then, seeing that the Bible gave him just what he needed, he began to study the Bible, and he began to believe it. He started family worship at home, and told people that he was no more a deist, but that he believed in Christ and in the Bible.

He read the Bible more and more, and cared less and less for other reading matter. The Bible became his guide, and Jesus became his friend.

A very important part of the Bible is its prophecies. Only God knows what is coming to pass in the future and exactly when it will be; [35]but in order that men need not be surprised, "surely," says Amos, "the Lord God will do nothing but He revealeth His secret unto His servants the prophets." Now William Miller, in studying the Bible, began to discover how God had spoken through

Preparing a Messenger

the prophets of things to come, and they had come just as the prophecies said.

In the book of the Prophet Daniel he read of the time when the Messiah (that is, Christ) should come; and true enough, Jesus the Christ did come at the

He read the Bible more and more.

time foretold, the beginning of [36] His ministry being in the year 27, and His crucifixion in the year 31. Then William Miller read in the same prophecy the time when "the sanctuary shall be cleansed," and that time, he found by figuring on the basis the prophecy gave, came in 1844.

What did it mean: "the sanctuary shall be cleansed"? Very few, if any, had studied the sanctuary question then, and so a great mistake was made. In common with nearly all Christians at that time, William Miller believed the sanctuary to be this earth, whereas we now know that the sanctuary of God is in heaven. But, believing as he did, William Miller came to the conclusion that the cleansing of the sanctuary meant the cleansing of this earth by fire. And as Peter tells us, the earth and all its works will be burned up when Jesus comes the second time. So Miller believed that the Lord Jesus would come in 1844.

When he first began to study this subject, it was about the year 1816; but for many years he waited, while still studying, thinking that he could never be called to teach or preach. For, as you remember, he was a farmer, not a preacher, and he could not think that he ought to go out and preach that the end of the world was near. He thought God would find [37] somebody else to do that. And so it came along to the year 1831. It was time for the second advent message to begin, and now it would begin, and William Miller was the man God was going to use to start it in America.

So here he sits on an August morning, at his desk in his east room, studying, when there come to his mind, as though God spoke them, the words: "Go and tell it to the world." He sinks into his chair, saying, "I can't go, Lord." [38]

Here he sits on an August morning studying the Bible.

"Why not?" comes the question.

"Oh, I'm not a preacher; I'm a plain farmer. I haven't the ability."

But that wouldn't do, and at last he thought he settled it by promising the Lord that if the Lord would open the way, then he would go.

"What do you mean by opening the way?" came the next question.

"Why," he said, "if I am asked to speak publicly in any place, I will go and tell them what I find in the Bible about the Lord's coming."

Then he felt all right and happy; for he thought nobody would ever ask him to speak. So he arose and prepared to go out to work. But before he was ready, there came a knock at the door. He opened it to find there his nephew, Irving Guilford, who had come with a message from his father in Dresden, sixteen miles away, down Lake Champlain. [39]

III

THE MESSAGE BEGINS

Morning worship was over in the Guilford family, but the boys and girls lingered to hear the outcome of a very interesting question.

"Sylvia," said Mr. Guilford, "couldn't we get William to come over, since the minister is away, and talk to us and the neighbors tomorrow about the coming of the Lord?"

"Oh," said his wife, who was William Miller's sister, "I'm afraid William wouldn't do it. You know he says he is no preacher. Of course he has talked to us and his neighbors about the prophecies, but be wouldn't speak in public."

"Well," returned Mr. Guilford, "he needn't preach. We'll gather the neighbors in here, and he can come and sit and talk with us. He can just talk to the neighbors, and that's enough. Why," and Mr. Guilford sat up in his armchair very vigorously, "if he believes that the Lord is coming about 1844, he has to tell it. The world must know."

"The prophecies are right, aren't they, Silas?" demanded Mrs. Guilford. [40]

"The prophecies are right," he answered, "and William's figures seem all right. That's why I want him to come and talk to us so we can all get it straightened out."

"You might send Irving over to see," she said. And at that, Irving, a tall sixteen-year-old boy, straightened up from the doorpost be had been leaning against, and stretched his hand up toward his cap-peg.

"Irving," said his father, "saddle the brown mare and ride over to Uncle William's. Tell him the Baptist minister is away, and we want him to come

"Hadn't I better cut across the lake, Pa, at Brennan's Landing?"

over for tomorrow and talk to us and the neighbors about the coming of the Lord."

"Hadn't I better cut across the lake, pa, at Brennan's Landing? I can get a boat there," said the boy.

"All right," said his father; "quickest way to get to Low Hampton."

"Breakfast is all ready," said Patience, the oldest girl, looking in from the lean-to kitchen.

"Can't wait for breakfast," answered Irving, as he bolted through the door. And that is how, galloping, galloping along the lakeshore, pulling, pulling at the oars with all the muscles of arms and legs and back, and cutting across country on foot the other side of the lake, be came to William Miller's with the [41] message of the work be must do just as Miller thought he had rolled off its burden.

"Father wants you to come over to our place tomorrow and talk to us on the coming of Christ," said the boy. "The minister is away, and we'll have all the neighbors come to our house, so you can have the whole church there."

Miller looked at the boy without speaking. He was thunderstruck. The Lord had taken him up on his promise. Without answering a word, he strode past the boy and out of the house. He walked down toward his grove, all the way the words sounding in his ears, "Go and tell it! Go and tell it!" When be reached the grove, he fell on his knees and prayed that the Lord would release him from his promise. But all the answer he received was, "Go and tell it to the world." He could not get away from it. He had promised that if he was called to speak in public, he would; and now, not half an hour afterward, he had the call.

"I will," he said at last in tears; and rising, he went back to the house, where Irving Guilford still waited. "I'll go with you," said William Miller to his nephew; and after dinner they started off, Miller's Bible and psalmbook under his arm.

The next day, Sunday, all the neighbors who [43] belonged to the Baptist church came flocking to the Guilford house, for all the little Guilfords had been sent around the neighborhood, telling the people to come and hear William Miller talk about the coming of the Lord. [44]

They crowded full the big room of the log house, sitting on quilt-covered

The Message Begins

"Father wants you to come over to our place tomorrow and talk to us on the coming of Christ."

boards stretched from chair to stool and from stool to woodblock. The children came with their fathers and mothers, the older ones crowding close to their parents, and the little ones sitting on mother's lap or standing at father's knee. So they waited, breathless, on that October morning for the talk that was to begin the giving of the second advent message in America.

William Miller sat in the big armchair, his sturdy body, now a little bent at the shoulders, amply filling it, his earnest eyes lighting up his square-chiseled face, as the points of his theme passed through his mind.

Pioneer Stories

They sang a hymn, and prayer was offered. And then William Miller, still sitting in the big armchair, read to the neighbors the message from Daniel. He showed them how the empires of Babylon, Medo-Persia, Grecia, and Rome had come and gone, as the prophecy showed under the symbols of the lion, the bear, the leopard, and the terrible beast with iron teeth; how the papal power, "the little horn," had oppressed and killed the saints of God for 1260 years; and how, 2300 years from the commandment to restore and to build Jerusalem, the sanctuary should be cleansed, which, as he said, and as [45] they all believed, meant the cleansing of the earth by fire.

And then William Miller, still sitting in the big armchair, read to the neighbors the message from Daniel.

The Message Begins

Then he showed them how that commandment went forth in 457 B.C., and he had them figure it themselves, and they saw it come out in 1843 or 1844. [46]

There was a little boy at that meeting who lived for half a century after, and he told me much of all this.

He remembered, oh, so distinctly, Uncle William Miller sitting there in the big armchair, talking about the coming of the Lord. And he remembered how, though Uncle William Miller was not preaching, but only telling very simply what the Bible told, there came into the meeting a power more than they had felt with any preacher before, and how the tears came to the eyes of strong men, and gentle women wept, and the children, whose ears and hearts had been open, understood the truth very well too, and they believed truly that Jesus was very soon coming.

After the meeting, some crowded around William Miller, asking him more about the beasts that meant kingdoms, and the days that meant years, and the sanctuary that was to be cleansed. Others went silently away, thinking, thinking very deeply. But they all, before they left, made Miller promise to stay and tell them more. You see he knew now that the Lord had set him to do this work, and he could not stop with just one talk. So for several days he stayed with his sister's family, and every day and every evening the people came, and he talked with them, and they believed. Many who had [47] been worldly were converted again, many who had been thought good and great confessed their sins and sought to get ready to meet Jesus, and children were brought to their Saviour.

The children used to hold little prayer meetings all alone by themselves, besides meeting with the older ones. Out into the groves they would go, not for a picnic, but to pray together that God would make their hearts clean, make them kind and loving and helpful to father and mother and brothers and sisters and playmates. A great work was done there in Dresden, for nearly every one of the church members, and many others, accepted Jesus as their Saviour, and began to prepare for His coming.

When William Miller reached home again after his visit, he found a letter waiting for him from a minister in Poultney, Vermont, where he used to live, asking him to come to that place and speak on the coming of Christ. He went, and there again many were brought to Jesus. And from this time on, William

Miller could not rest, for from everywhere people were calling for him to speak to them. Of course there were people to make fun of him and what be taught, men who would call him hard names and tell lies about him, ministers who did not really love Jesus and who did not want Him to come, who [48] tried to prove William Miller wrong. But still the work grew, and thousands were converted. Many men who had been infidels, or deists like Miller himself, were led to believe the Bible true, for they saw its prophecies had been fulfilled, and hundreds of them confessed their belief in the Bible and in Jesus, and began to look for His appearing. [49]

But still the work grew, and thousands were converted.

IV

THE MESSAGE SPREADS

For several years William Miller, though he awakened great interest in New York, New England, and Canada, and though he saw many people converted and added to the different churches, yet had to work alone. But in 1839, he preached in the city of Boston, Massachusetts, at the church of a young minister by the name of Joshua V. Himes. This young man believed what Mr. Miller taught about the coming of the Lord, and he wanted the message to go much farther and faster.

"Do you really believe," he asked Miller after the sermon, "do you really believe what you preach about the coming of the Lord?"

"Of course I do," answered William Miller, "or I would not preach it."

"Well, then," said Himes, "what are you doing to give it to the world? The big cities ought to hear it."

"I am doing what I can."

"Well," said Himes, "the whole thing is kept in a corner yet. After all you have done, very few know of it. If Christ is to come in a few [50] years, no time should be lost in telling the world."

"I know it, I know it, Brother Himes," said Mr. Miller, "but what can an old farmer do?" and he spread his hands in a gesture of despair. "I have been looking for someone to take hold of the message and help give it; but though the ministers seem glad to have me come and preach and add people to their churches, no one has ever offered to help give the message."

"Well," said Himes, "will you go with me where doors are open?"

"Do you really believe," asked Himes, *"that the Lord is coming?"*

The Message Spreads

"I am willing to go anywhere and work my hardest to the end," he answered.

And from that time on, Joshua Himes began traveling with Father Miller,— as he was now called, because of his kind and fatherly ways and because he was old. The work moved much faster, and many more men came in to give the message. There were Charles Fitch, who planned and made the first prophetic charts, such as I am sure you have all seen; and Josiah Litch, and Henry Dana Ward, and Elon Galusba, and George Storrs, a popular evangelist in New York City, and Joseph Bates, who had been a sea captain, and now was to be a greater captain in the army of the Lord; and there came at last to be hundreds of preachers. [52]

Himes proposed to start a paper to tell the message. But he was as poor as the rest were. Father Miller had been having pamphlets published to give away, and had been paying all his own traveling expenses, and what little money he had was eaten up almost faster than he got it. They wanted the paper, but how could they get money to print it? But as Himes told the people about how anxious he was to start the paper, one day an old man, a sea captain from the state of Maine, stepped up and handed him a silver dollar. "Here's a dollar for the paper, Brother [53] Himes," said he. That one dollar was the first in a fund

"Here's a dollar for the paper, Brother Himes."

35

with which Himes started a paper called, *The Signs of the Times*, and very soon this paper was going everywhere, telling the message.

In those days they started camp meetings. Camp meetings were new then. The Methodists seem to have started them first, a few years before, in the West, where people had to come to a camp meeting to hear a preacher at all. They would come from a hundred miles around, to stay for two or three days to hear the minister preach. They camped out in the woods, in booths or wigwams made of poles and branches, and the meetings were held outdoors. Then, when they began to have them in the East, in New England and New York and other places, some people took tents with them, in which several families lived, separated by curtains, while others camped outdoors. And the meetings were held outdoors still, around a rough platform built for the ministers.

And this was the kind of camp meeting the believers in Jesus' coming began to have all through the land. Sometimes as many as ten thousand people would be gathered together, all quiet and orderly; for they came to hear the terrible and wonderful and glad tidings of the coming of Jesus. The new advent hymns that [54] were beginning to be sung added great power to the preaching. Do you know any of those hymns? You can find some of them in the "Church Hymnal," from No. 659 to No. 670. One of the most beautiful ones is No. 338, written by Charles Fitch. It begins:

> "One precious boon, O Lord, I seek,
> While tossed upon life's billowy sea:
> To hear a voice within me speak,
> 'Thy Saviour is well pleased with thee.'"

Those that the people sang more often, perhaps, making the air ring with the deep chorus, were like this one:

> "Hear the glorious proclamation,
> The glad tidings of salvation,
> Hear the glorious proclamation
> Of the Saviour near.

"While the heavenly choir of angels,
While the heavenly choir of angels,
While the heavenly choir of angels
Shall be chanting through the sky."

From east and west, north and south, people were sending in letters asking for preachers to come and tell them of the message. Miller and [55] Himes visited Philadelphia, and Washington, the capital of the country, and hundreds of other towns. And the other ministers, many of whose names we do not now know, were at work in almost every town in the Northern states. People in the South were calling for them, in Charleston, S.C., in Savannah, Ga., and Mobile, Ala., and many other places. William Miller could not go on to these places, because he had promised to go to so many others, but some ministers did go into the South. A little later we shall have the story of how two carried the message to both slaves and white people.

At this time, too, the believers in America began to hear how the message was going all over the world. They heard of Joseph Wolff in Asia, of Edward Irving in England, and of the messengers in many other places. A missionary turning from the Holy Land told them they were hearing the message there, and sea captains told of being asked about it at every port where they stopped, and of finding books and papers. It was found before long that the message was indeed going to every part of the earth. [56]

V

IN THE WEST

The cold December winds drove the snow against the window where sat a minister looking out with troubled eyes and prayerful mind. Charles Fitch knew not where to go nor what to do. He felt as though he were shut up in some narrow prison cell, prevented from giving to the people the bread and water of life which the Lord had put into his hands to feed them. His keen blue eyes, so happy always, were misty, now with tears. His ready smile had given way to a frown of perplexity. His fingers turned the pages of his Bible uncertainly as he sought for direction of his course.

Yet be was not in prison; he was in his own home at Haverhill, Massachusetts, and though be was alone, his wife and children being in New York City visiting their friends, Dr. and Mrs. Palmer, it was not because he was lonesome that he felt so sad. No; it was because there seemed no way open for him to preach his message any more to the people. Now his mind went over his experience since his school days, seeking to assure himself again of the Lord's leadings. Since he [57] came out from Brown University fifteen years before, he had been a true and beloved pastor in different churches of Connecticut and Massachusetts, last of all in Boston in the Marlboro Chapel, a Congregational church. Here in 1838 he had first heard of William Miller and his preaching of the coming of Christ, and he wrote him a letter asking for printed copies of his lectures. But though he had then studied the subject and his mind had been overwhelmed with the evidences of the Lord's coming, he had not pursued the course it opened to him. Soon he had left his Boston church and was traveling widely, preaching through

In the West

New England and New York, even to Buffalo on Lake Erie, then in the new and undeveloped West. Now, in 1841, he was back in Massachusetts, at Haverhill, some forty miles north of Boston.

But it seemed the doors of the churches now were shut to him. Where should he go to tell the message of God's love and desire to make His people perfect in His love? He had fasted and prayed and wept before the Lord, but no way was open for him to continue.

Then as he sat there this cold December day, there came a knock at his door. When he opened it, there stepped within a stranger who said, "Brother Fitch, you do not know me, but I [58] have known of you for four years, since you first inquired about the message of the Lord's coming. For in that year I also heard this faith, and believed it, and began to preach it. My name is Josiah Litch, of Philadelphia."

"Brother Fitch, you need the truth of the coming of Jesus."

Then they talked together, and as Fitch told his new friend of his perplexities, Litch said to him, "Brother, you need the truth of Jesus' coming with the message you have been preaching."

Pioneer Stories

Charles Fitch turned again to his Bible and studied the subject of Jesus' coming. And again he was convinced, and now he put his whole [59] soul into it. He expected, as did others who accepted this faith, that he would lose his friends, some of whom in his ministry of love had become very dear to him. And, of course, there were some who turned against him, but there were others who rejoiced with him in the faith of Jesus' coming. Among the dearest of these were the ones whom his family were visiting, Dr. W. C. Palmer and his wife, Phoebe Palmer, who afterward wrote many second advent hymns, among them that stirring song, "Jesus Comes." ("*Church Hymnal*," No. 549.)

"Watch, ye saints, with eyelids waking;
Lo! the powers of heaven are shaking;
Keep your lamps all trimmed and burning,
Ready for your Lord's returning.
Lo! He comes!
Lo! Jesus comes.

"Nations wane, though proud and stately;
Christ His kingdom hasteneth greatly;
Earth her latest pangs is summing;
Shout, ye saints, your Lord is coming.
Lo! He comes!
Lo! Jesus comes."

Now speedily Charles Fitch found the ears of the people open to listen, and with Miller and [60] Himes and Litch and others, he went forth to proclaim the soon coming of Jesus. It took him far away from his home most of the time. To travel by foot and horse and stage and steamboat was hard; there was no certain pay; but there was gladness in his heart and voice as he went out to give the message.

Very soon, as he was lecturing on the visions of Daniel and John, there came to his mind a word from the prophet Habakkuk, "Write the vision, and make it plain upon tables, that he may run that readeth it," and he sat down and devised the first prophetic charts. I know that you are familiar with these

Charles Fitch made the first prophetic chart.

charts, which are used so widely now, and which make so vivid the meanings of the prophecies; and you may remember whenever you see them that the one who first planned them was Charles Fitch.

In the latter part of 1842 Charles Fitch started for the West to proclaim the message. In those times the United States was not so large as now, and the territory beyond the Appalachian Mountains and around the Great Lakes was very little settled. There were as yet no railroads out there, but the rivers and the Great Lakes were beginning to be used by steamboats; and two canals in the state of Ohio, which connected Lake Erie with the Ohio River, had [61] helped greatly to develop the country. Cincinnati, then the largest city, had about forty thousand people, and Cleveland on Lake Erie had about six thousand.

Fitch went to Cleveland, where he soon moved his family, and where he lived for the next two years. From this place, he, with Elon Galusha and other ministers, went out over the state to the new and growing cities and the little towns where the country people would come in to listen to the message. Akron and Marietta, the oldest town in the state, were cities where the message was gladly received, and indeed all through this Western country the preachers of the advent message found a people more ready to believe in Jesus' coming than those in the older country of the East. These new settlers were deeply interested in education also, and they established schools like Oberlin College, near Cleveland, where the students and some of the teachers largely supported themselves on the farm and in other industries, and where a true Christian education was in every way encouraged. At Oberlin there was great interest in the message which Charles Fitch and his helpers brought, and many there turned to look for the coming of their Lord.

In Cleveland, Fitch found a Congregational [63] church, which was willing to let him use their building, fronting the public square, and from this church for perhaps a year the people of Cleveland in greater and greater numbers heard the message proclaimed. Finally the company of believers built a larger church, in which the work was continued. One who was then a young man living in Cleveland, has told me of hearing Charles Fitch preach. "He was a very winsome man," he said, "slender, but well built, and with a smile that would disarm an enemy and which truly spoke the kindliness of his nature. He was a very powerful speaker, and under his preaching many nights I have seen hundreds, deeply convicted, rise and go forward to ask for prayers and salvation in the kingdom. There was a solemnity about the meetings that none, even of the most flippant, could resist or change. Fitch had always command of his audiences.

"One night, I remember, when at the close of his sermon he called for repentant sinners to come forward, a great lubberly fellow, whom I well knew, with others rose in the gallery and started to come down the stairs which led to the pulpit. Part way down he stumbled and almost fell the rest of the way. A laugh started among the lighter-minded in the audience, but Mr. Fitch called out, 'Never mind, brother! It's [64] better to stumble into heaven than to walk straight into hell.' And the laughing died as quickly as it had started."

In this church the people of Cleveland heard the message.

In the summer of 1844 William Miller, to whom Charles Fitch was very dear, came on a tour of the cities and country where Fitch had been working. He came to Cleveland preached there, and then went on to other cities [65] and towns as far as Cincinnati. And everywhere he found the people in great crowds eager to hear.

Not only did Fitch preach, but he published in Cleveland a paper called, *The Second Advent of Christ*, which for two years carried far out through the northwestern country the message which he could not everywhere carry in person. A great love of the truth of Jesus' near coming was thus planted in the hearts of the people; and, as you shall see, in later years the fruit of this sowing was reaped in the rapid progress of the message.

Charles Fitch, however, did not have long thereafter to labor. You will find a most interesting statement about his death and his coming reward in "Early Writings," on page 17, fifteenth edition. The cause of his death, in October, 1844, was a fever which was brought on in the following way. He had a large number of new believers who desired baptism, and others who had not yet made up their minds. The company who were ready went with him to the lake, and there were baptized. A cold wind was blowing as he, with them, started in his wet garments for home, and he was much chilled. But he had not gone far when he met another company from among those whom he had left behind, who now came desiring baptism. He went back with them [66] to the lake and also immersed them. Then as they started home there came a third company whose conviction of sin and of Jesus' salvation and of His soon coming had brought them to the decision. At their request he turned again and baptized them also. The next day, though ill from the effects of his chill, he rode in the cold wind some miles to another appointment. This proved too hard on him, and he was stricken down, and after an illness of several weeks he died. His last clear words, in answer to some who asked him of his faith, were, "I believe in the promises of God."

Among all those in America who preached and taught the message of Jesus' coming, perhaps none was so widely and deeply loved as Charles Fitch. He had a depth of love, which reached high to his Saviour and low and far to his fellow men. Always courageous, hopeful, and helpful, he interpreted the love of God not only in word but in deed, and he bound firmly in friendship and perfect love thousands to whom he ministered and hundreds with whom he labored. He did a great work, and he left a mark of his labors both upon the country where he preached and upon the methods of his successors. He may well be remembered as "The Beloved Apostle of the Advent Message." [67]

VI

IN THE SOUTH

There was not much to do at the store, but the loungers cared little for that. The weather was cold for Maryland; there had even been a little snow, and Chesapeake Bay was filled with ice. There was no horse racing, no cockfighting, no shipwreck; so naturally the idlers in this part of Kent Island drifted to the rum store.

It was the place where all the vile and the lazy were used to meeting. Merica's tavern in the town was a temperance place, something not very often found in those days. Men could get no rum or whisky there; so the keeper of this little crossroads store, two miles out in the country, had found it paid to keep the wicked stuff for men to drink.

There were flabby old men there, and blear-eyed sots, and boys from whose cheeks and eyes rum had not yet wholly driven away the freshness. And they gathered around the cracked stove, sitting on casks and kegs and the remains of a chair or two, or lounging on the long, bare wooden counter; and every once in awhile, urged by their false thirst or by the liquor dealer's [68] voice, they stopped to drink down the fiery West Indian rum or the cheaper corn whisky of their own land.

Very soon the talk turned upon the two "Millerites" who they had heard were coming to preach the end of the world. They hooted at the idea; and the more afraid of it one was, the more boastingly he talked, just as a scary boy, going through a graveyard in the dark of night, whistles to make everyone think he's not afraid.

The idlers drifted to the rum store.

But as they drank deeper and talked louder, they grew wilder, and began to threaten what they would do to the men who had come to tell them what they didn't want to hear. And at [69] last, among them, they hatched a plot to catch the preachers, tar and feather them, and ride them on a rail to the bay, or as far as the mob might feel like going.

News of their plot floated out on the wings of rumor to Merica's tavern, where the two preachers had arrived the night before. As the drunken fellows lurched up to the tavern, they found a large crowd outside, discussing the message that these men were supposed to be bringing. None there were ready to stand up for it, and they only vied with one another in seeing who could deride it most.

Besides, they said, these Millerites were black-hearted Abolitionists, who had come down from New England to get away the slaves of the Southerners, and make trouble generally. You know in that time nearly all the black people in our country were slaves, who worked for their masters all their lives, and got no pay, only they were given a home and their food and clothing. Some of the masters were very kind to their slaves, and their slaves loved them. But of course there were many bad men, too, who owned slaves, and they acted toward their slaves very much as some children I have known act toward their pet birds and animals. You know these animals are our slaves. And if a boy [70] kicks his dog and pounds and scolds his horse, and if a little girl forgets to keep her birdcage clean and sweet, or to give food and water to her chickens, how do you think our slaves feel? What kind of slave-master do you think such a boy or girl would have made?

But of course God never meant a man or a woman to be a slave. Some good people didn't realize this then, and some people who did realize it didn't want to give up the slaves; for they would lose money if they should. And so most of the slave-masters were afraid to have their slaves learn anything about liberty; that is, about being free. And they feared that if the slaves heard Jesus was coming and would set them free, they would all break out and do terrible things even before He did come. So from some places where the ministers had been to preach, the slave-owners had driven them out.

An Abolitionist was one who knew slavery was wrong and believed it ought to be stopped. Some of them did very rash and wrong things in trying to get it stopped and to have the slaves set free, but they were nearly all honest and very good men, nevertheless, who were stirred up by the wrongs the slaves had to endure.

The mob for the time fell apart, pushing and sidling their way through the crowd. One of [71] them brought up at last near where two men were discussing the matter. One, a Mr. Kent, was making fun of the message, and declaring that the men who preached it were crazy or else fools. Any man, he declared, could show its foolishness in a minute. But Doctor Harper was not so sure. "Wait and see," was all he answered. Mr. Kent, however, would not wait, but went on ridiculing the idea that Jesus was coming soon.

The drunken man at his elbow was sympathetic. This was what he liked to hear. "We'll settle 'em, Kent," he exclaimed, familiarly; "got a hunerd of us here as'll tar an' feather 'em."

Mr. Kent turned to look at his helper, turned and stared, and turned back again without a word. He wasn't seeking for such help, he thought. This sort was below him, but he would settle himself when they came to preach.

Just then from within the tavern came a clear baritone voice singing:

"O sweet are the tidings that greet the pilgrim's ear,
As he wanders in exile from home!
Soon, soon will the Saviour in glory appear,
And soon the kingdom come."

At that the crowd began pushing their way into the hall of the tavern. The singer soon [72] stopped, and sat down, and a tall man, straight as an Indian, stood up to speak. His clear blue eye, fearless, commanding, yet with a kindness that made it mild, passed slowly over the crowd and stilled them into quiet.

"O sweet are the tidings that greet the pilgrim's ear."

"What's his name?" whispered a man who found himself next the tavern keeper.

"Captain Bates," replied Mr. Merica. "He was shipwrecked near my father's when I was a [73] boy. Mother knew him first laid on him."

Joseph Bates had begun to speak. He was quoting Scripture which many didn't catch, for there was yet a little confusion, and most eyes, besides, were fixed upon a chart hanging behind him, on which were printed in black and gold and red, pictures of strange beasts and a crowned man with arms folded. They wanted to hear about that, and very soon they heard, for Bates began to tell them of the prophecies of Daniel, the image of gold, silver, brass, iron, and clay that Nebuchadnezzaer saw, and Daniel's vision of the beasts that mean Babylon, Medo-Persia, Greece, and Rome. And through the eighth and ninth chapters he brought them, and showed them how, as he believed, since the sanctuary would be cleansed in 1843 or 1844, the Lord Jesus would come at that time, and that was only a few months away. He pleaded with them all to get ready to meet Jesus.

Many were deeply moved by what he said, but Mr. Kent was not. No sooner was the lecture finished than he rose and began to abuse the speaker and the message. "I can put it all down in ten minutes," he shouted.

Joseph Bates, who was still standing up, in [74] that straight, strong way of his, said quietly, "We will hear you."

So he tried to prove it all wrong, but of course, since be was all wrong himself, he couldn't do very well, and pretty soon he became confused and stopped. But that only made him angry; and, ready now to take the help of the fellows he had scorned before, he looked around for their support, and declared, "We'll ride you out of town on a rail." He thought he would scare those preachers.

But Bates smiled and said pleasantly, "We're all ready for that, sir.If you'll put a saddle on it, we had rather ride than walk."

The man looked around again, but be saw only smiling faces or shamed faces; for no one could do anything dreadful to a man who took it all as a joke. Then Bates said to him seriously,

"You must not think we have come six hundred miles through the snow and ice, at our own expense, to lecture to you, without first sitting down and counting the cost.And now, if the Lord has no more for us to do, we had as lief lie at the bottom of Chesapeake Bay as anywhere else, until the Lord comes.

Joseph Bates said quietly, "We will hear you."

But if He has any more work for us to do, you can't touch us."

Up leaped Dr. Harper. "You know better, Kent," he said; "you ought to be ashamed of [75] yourself. This man has been giving us the truth from the Bible, and I believe it." And immediately others began to show how they sided with the preachers; and the mob from the rum store and the men like Mr. Kent had no chance to do the mean and cowardly things they had planned to do.

Mr. Gurney stood up and sang some more hymns, and Joseph Bates sang with him. Wonderful power those advent hymns had in those days, and many there were after the singing who came up to ask the ministers to pray with them and for them.

The Negro slaves were very anxious to hear, and at meetings in other places, later than this, they would come when their masters would let them; and after the white people had taken their places, the slaves would crowd in, making a black fringe all around the outside. They were wonderfully pleased with the advent songs Mr. Gurney sang. Here is one they especially delighted in:

"I'm a pilgrim, and I'm a stranger;
I can tarry, I can tarry but a night;
Do not detain me, for I am going
To where the fountains are ever flowing.
I'm a pilgrim, and I'm a stranger;
I can tarry, I can tarry but a night. [77]

"There's the city to which I journey;
My Redeemer, my Redeemer is its light!
There is no sorrow, nor any sighing,
Nor any tears there, nor any dying.
I'm a pilgrim, and I'm a stranger;
I can tarry, I can tarry but a night."

When they preached at Chestertown, an aged black man followed them after the meeting to their lodging place, to beg for a copy of that song. Mr. Gurney had only one, and he couldn't give it up.

"I'll give you a quarter for it," said the poor fellow,—probably all the

In the South

money he had in the world. At last Mr. Gurney made him a copy, and he went away with it delighted.

Often after the service Bates and Gurney would talk with the slaves, who had to wait until all the white people had passed out.

"Could you hear what was said?" they were asked.

"Yes, massa, ebery word," they answered.

"Do you believe?"

"Yes, massa, b'leve it all."

"Don't you want some tracts?"

"Yes, massa."

"But can you read?"

"No, massa, but young missus or massa's son [78] will read for us" And they took the tracts that told of the signs of Jesus' coming, so not only they, but their masters who read to them, received the message. And they looked with joy for Jesus to come, when they should be set free. There were true Christians among them, for some of the Christian slave-owners had been faithful in teaching their servants about Jesus; and many of these poor black people by their lives put to shame the white people who did not so well as they. Do you think the Lord loved them, though oftentimes they went in rags, and though they knew only a little of the truth? And will He remember them when He comes to raise His children from the dead?

During their stay in the South, Bates and Gurney found many who believed the truth they were preaching. Some of the slave-owners believed and were so anxious to have their slaves hear that they commanded them all to come, every single one. Men who had been infidels and Universalists acknowledged they were wrong and that the Bible was right, and they turned to get ready for the Lord. So a great awakening occurred in that part of Maryland. And this is an example of the way the work went in the South. [79]

VII

IN THE NORTH

The brown horse trotted along well content, notwithstanding his bridle was wondrously patched and his saddle old and worn, while the man upon his back, though young enough, wore clothes as well patched as the harness. He was a messenger of the King, and though we may not suppose that the horse knew anything of that, he did know that his master was kind and thoughtful toward him, and he was willing to carry a man anywhere who would be as good to him as this young preacher.

They were traveling, James White and his horse, from their home in central Maine, to Augusta, the capital of the state. It was cold, for it was in January. The horse kept warm enough, trotting over the frozen, snowy road, but his rider shivered under his thin overcoat as the keen blast whistled around them. Warm memories they were, however, that we may believe coursed through his mind, going over his experiences thus far.

Coming home from teaching, two years before, he had been astonished to hear his mother [80] tell him of the message that was being preached of Jesus' coming. He did not want to believe, but as he tried to show the doctrine wrong, he found his mother more than a match for him, for she had truth on her side. And quietly she interested him in it, until he gave up all for it.

And now, with a warmer glow, would come the thought of his first mission; how the Lord had sent him, against his will, back to his school pupils, to pray with them; how, as he tramped along on his errand that bright spring morning, [81] the peace of God had come into his heart and blessed him, and made him able, little as he knew, to begin to gather people into the fold of Christ.

They were traveling to Augusta.

After that he had studied hard to get ready to give the truth; for he had not been much of a Bible student before, and he realized that he must thoroughly know the prophecies and their meaning, as well as the rest the Bible, if he was going to help people.

Poor enough, he thought, had been his efforts to preach that message, but God had been with him, and helped him teach the people.

The stinging cold at last drew back his thoughts to the present, and he found he was nearing the city of Augusta. The night was coming on, and he did not know of any friend in the city. But as he came to the outskirts, he saw a humble little cottage, and getting down from his horse, he walked up to the door, knocked, and said to the man who opened it: "I am a penniless preacher, and I am looking for a place to stay with some good Christian family, who will care for me and my horse without charge."

"Come in," said the man, "I'm a member the Christian church of this place, and you may stay with me." So he had found a friend at the very first. Who do you think led him there? [82]

That evening the man told him that Elder Pearl was going to preach next Sunday.

"Elder Pearl!" exclaimed James White; "why, I know him," and he felt he was more than ever among friends. He told his new friend what he was out for, to give message of Jesus' coming in 1844, and as he told him something of the truth, the man's heart warmed, and he said he would arrange for him to give some lectures in the schoolhouse. This he did, and Elder Pearl, whom Mr. White found next day, stayed with him and helped him.

But there seemed a good opening in the school district a mile east of the city, where be was invited to come and give lectures. So within a week we find him out there. There was a good interest. So many wanted to hear, that the schoolhouse was packed, and though it was winter, many stood outside at the open windows to listen. A good many, of course, did not want to hear the message, and were bound to break the meetings up.

A Universalist editor was brought to oppose, and after young Mr. White had finished his first lecture, this Universalist wanted the people to stay and hear *him* tell how it all wasn't so. But it was late; and besides, James White, knowing how inexperienced he was, was afraid he could [83] not stand up against a learned man like this editor. He was not afraid the truth could not win, but that he did not know enough of the truth to show it. So he told the people he would not keep them, and he left. All but a few rough fellows went with him, leaving the Universalist almost alone. This made him angry, and he had those ruffians agree to break up the meeting the next night.

When it came time to go to the meeting, Mr. White's friends came and told him there was a mob of at least three hundred around the schoolhouse, and that they would kill him. He went by himself and prayed, and then he felt that the Lord would protect him if he would go. His friends went with him.

They found the schoolhouse filled with women, all the windows out, and

In the North

hundreds of men around the house. Amid yells and catcalls, he pressed through the fear-stricken company within, up to the desk. The Universalist stood near the desk, and he said, "Your meeting will be broken up, because you acted as you did last night."

"Very well, sir," responded James White, "if it is the will of God."

He stood up and prayed, not daring to close his eyes, for the angry Universalist seemed ready [84] to strike him. A snowball whistled by his head, and spattered on the wall behind.

The mob were yelling, snowballs were flying.

He read the text from Second Peter which prophesies of the destruction of the world, and began to tell the people about it. But the mob were yelling, snowballs were flying, very few could hear him, his Bible and his clothes were wet with the melted fragments of the snowballs that burst on the walls around. So he closed his Bible, and raising his voice [85] above the noise of the mob, he began to describe the terrible scenes of the judgment day. God gave him a wonderful sight of those scenes, gave him language to describe them, and power of voice to make himself heard.

"Repent and be converted," he cried, "that your sins may he blotted out, or you will drink of the wrath of God. Turn to Christ, and get ready for His coming, or in a little from this, on rocks and mountains you will call in vain. You scoff now, but you will pray then."

The mob grew quiet. Putting his hand into his pocket, James White brought out a big nail, which had been thrown at him and hit him on the forehead the night before.

"Some poor sinner cast this spike at me last evening," he said. "God pity him. The worst wish I have for him is that he is at this moment as happy as I am. Why should I resent this insult when my Master had them driven through His hands?" and stepping back, he raised his arms, and placed them on the wall behind him, like one hanging on a cross.

The Spirit of God struck the hearts of that great company. Some shrieked, others groaned.

"Hark, hark!" many cried.

Out of the confusion the young preacher's voice was rising clear, telling of the love of God, [86] and calling on sinners to come to Him. The people sobbed and cried, while he still talked to them. None were cursing or yelling now.

"Who are willing to seek Christ," he asked, "and with me suffer persecution and be ready for His coming? Who in this crowd wish me to pray for them, that this may be their happy lot? As many as do, please rise."

From all over the house they rose to their feet, nearly a hundred of them. It was late, and the young preacher was hoarse and weary. He [87] prayed for them, and then, taking his chart and Bible, he stepped down and went out through the quiet crowd.

As he passed out of the door, someone stepped up and locked arms with him, to guard him through the mob. He did not know the man, though some-

In the North

how his noble, commanding face seemed familiar. Not one touched him as he passed through their midst. As soon as he was clear of the crowd, he turned to speak to his guard; but he was gone. From that evening he never found out who he was, nor where he went, nor how he left him. Was it not an angel sent from God to protect him? So in the very last days will angels, appearing as men, defend God's people from their enemies who would kill them. [99]

Someone stepped up to guard him through the mob.

VIII

HERALD TO ENGLAND

"Come out with me into the fields," said Irving to Frere. "I would like to talk with you about the things of Christ where we may be alone, with no one to disturb us." So the two left the company of their friends, and walked out together. And there in the fields that evening, as they walked and talked together, was born the second advent movement in old England.

Edward Irving was at that time the greatest preacher in all the British Isles. But at that he was the most humble and lovable of men. Born in Scotland thirty-three years before, he had now been for four years pastor of the most popular church in London. The members of his church were at first mostly lowly and common people; but before he had been preaching long, the lords and ladies and princes of England were flocking to hear him. And when he went on his journeys in England and into Scotland, great crowds thronged him, so that sometimes he preached to as many as ten thousand people out in the fields. He had the most wonderful voice, which he had trained to reach the farthest hearer, [89] while yet to those close at hand it was natural and pleasant. People said that his voice was like the music of many waters—now quietly murmuring like the brook, now rolling like the waves upon the seashore, and again thundering like a mighty waterfall.

He loved to go among the common people, and he helped them as Jesus did. He was tall and commanding in stature, with dark eyes, and [90] wavy black hair that fell to his shoulders; his smile and his voice were so winsome that he won the hearts of all he met. Often from his small store of money, he fed the hungry, clothed the naked, ministered to the sick. He held the children upon his knees—often dirty and unkempt children of the poor in the great cities of Glasgow and London; he told them stories, sang to them, and blessed them. He took the sick and the friendless into his own home, and Christian wayfarers found always a welcome there. He and his wife took care of all who came, and when their house overflowed with guests, Irving had many friends and followers who imitated him and took the needy in. Everywhere he went, crowds gathered around him, to listen to his words.

Irving asked Frere to walk with him in the fields.

This was the great Irving, to whom came a man but little known, James Hatley Frere, with a message which he felt sure was given of God, but to which he could get no one to listen. That message was of Jesus' coming. Frere had studied the prophecies, and he had been trying to have men of England listen to his message; but though he had talked and though he had written a book upon the subject, he seemed to make no progress at all.

"If only," said Frere to himself, "if only I might meet a man with an open and thoughtful [91] mind who yet has great influence with the public, so that they will listen to him and believe him, then I might talk to him and convince him of the truth of these prophecies that Jesus is soon coming. And he would convince the world."

And then Frere was invited to a gathering at a home of friends where Irving also came. They were introduced, and within a few minutes so welcome had they become to each other that Irving gave his invitation, "Come out with me into the fields, and let us talk of the things of Christ." Gravely listening, and asking only a few questions, Irving considered while Frere opened to his mind the prophecies of Jesus' coming. It was not all new to Irving; for he was a man who walked closely with his Lord and who felt Jesus' presence very near in his seasons of prayer and ministry. But he had not known the interpretation of the books of Daniel and Revelation, which foretold the history of the world and the coming of Christ.

Now when Frere opened to him the evidences from the Bible and from history that the second advent of the Lord Jesus Christ was very near, Irving's heart thrilled to the thought that the Lord with whom he so constantly communed was very soon to be revealed in His glorious person, and his eyes should look upon Him. At first, it is [92] true, the enthusiasm of Hatley Frere made him seem, as Irving afterward wrote him, "as one who dreamed, while you opened in my ear your views of the present time, as foretold in the hook of Daniel and the Apocalypse"—which is the book of Revelation. "But," said Irving humbly, "being ashamed of my own ignorance, and having been blessed from my youth with the desire of instruction, I dared not scoff at what I heard, but resolved to consider the matter." And consider he did, and study.

This was in the year 1825, which, as you note, was six years before William Miller began to teach in America. The following year, 1826, just when a grand new church which his friends were building for him in Regent's Square, London, was about ready, Irving with Frere and Henry Drummond called a great conference for study of the prophecies in the country home of Drummond, Albury Park. There were forty-four present, the larger number of them ministers, but some, like Drummond, men from the Parliament, or the army, or other laymen who were earnest Christians. Joseph Wolff, of whom you shall hear in the next story, was invited to be there. He came first to the home of Irving, whom he had never before met; and he tells how astonished he was at the tender care the great [93] Irving showed him. When Wolff asked for a servant to shave him, Irving, who had no servant, came himself and shaved him, at which all London laughed and sneered; but Wolff felt like Peter when the Saviour washed his feet.

Irving, who had no servant, came himself to shave him.

At this Albury Conference in 1826, the Rev. Hugh MacNeile presided. Besides him there were eighteen other clergymen of the Church of England (Episcopalians), four from Irving's [94] own Church of Scotland (Presbyterians), and three other ministers. Here they studied and prayed for six days, and says Irving, "The sweetest spot was the council room where I met the servants of the Lord—wise virgins waiting with oil in their lamps for the Bridegroom; and a sweeter still was that secret chamber where I met in the spirit my Lord and Master, whom I hope soon to meet in the flesh"

From this conference these men went out to preach and teach and print the message of Jesus' coming. Joseph Wolff went away to Asia and Africa and parts of Europe and even America. But the most, with Irving, stayed in their own land and preached the message. Many joined them, so that it is said there were at one time seven hundred clergymen of the Church of England alone, besides many of the other churches, who were giving this advent message.

Into the great new church in Regent's Square crowded thousands to hear the message Irving now had to give. His was a very busy life. Not only had he to preach, not only had he to counsel and advise many other ministers who looked to him as leader, not only was he busy with writing pamphlets and books, but every day he gave many hours in his own home, or in the homes of the people, to helping his people, [95] praying with them and teaching them; and besides this, he found many poor people, outcasts, drunkards, and sick, whom he sought out in the dens and slums of the city, often paying their bills or their fines from his own scanty purse, clothing them and feeding them, sometimes taking them into his own home to restore them. It was such a life as Jesus lived.

Irving loved children, as he had shown in his early ministry in Glasgow when he put his hands upon their heads and blessed them, and as he showed in London from the day when, praying for orphans, he first attracted the nobility of England, to the day when, cast out from his church, and preaching to the poor in the fields, he lifted a little lost and sobbing boy in his arms and comforted him until at the end of the sermon his mother found him. And Irving was very happy with his own family, though sorrow entered there to break the joy. He had married the next year after coming to London, but his first child, little Edward, was scarcely more than a year old when he died. His father and mother had gone with him back to the old home in Scotland, and there the mother stayed for a time, while Irving had to go back to his work. This was just at the time when he was beginning to study the prophecies. He wrote a [97] wonderfully beautiful journal, or series of letters "to comfort little Edward's mother," telling her first of his travels as he returned home, and then of his work, his visits, and his love. In his first letter he writes of his journey:

"I was lonely enough; but, committing my way unto the Lord, I held south

Into the great new church crowded thousands to hear Irving's message.

as nearly as I could guess, and reached the solitary house in the head of another water, of which Sam may recollect something; where, foregathering with a shepherd, I got directions, and set my breast against Blackhouse heights, and reached my old haunts on Douglas Burn, where, in answer to the apostolic benediction which I carried everywhere, I received a kindly offer of tea, night's lodging, then a horse to carry me through the wet, all of which in my haste refusing, I took my way over the rough grounds which lie between that and Dryhope by Loch St. Mary. My adventures here with the Inverness-shire herds and the dogs of Dryhope Tower (a perfect colony, threatening to devour me with open mouth), I cannot go into, and leave it to the discourse of the lip. Here I waded the narrow at the foot of the loch [lake], under the crescent moon, where, finding a convenient rock beneath some overhanging branches, which moaned and sighed in the breeze, I sat me down, while the wind, [98] sweeping, brought the waters of the loch to my feet, and I paid my devotions to the Lord in His own ample and magnificent temple, and sweet meditations were afforded me of thee, our babe, and our departed boy. My soul was filled with sweetness. 'I did not ask for a sign,' as Colonel Blackadder says; but when I looked up to the moon, as I came out from the ecclesia [church] of the rock, she looked as never a moon had looked before in my eye—as if she had been washed in dew, which, speedily clearing off, she looked so bright and beautiful; and on the summit of the opposite hill a little bright star gleamed upon me, like the bright, bright eye of our darling. Oh, how I wished you had been with me to partake of the sweet solacement of that moment! Of my adventure with the shepherd-boy Andrew, whose mother's sons were all squandered abroad among the shepherds, and our prayer upon the edge of the mountain, and my welcome at the cottage, and cold reception at the farmhouse, I must also be silent till the living pen shall declare them unto you. Only I had trial of an apostolic day and night, and slept sweetly, after blessing my wife and child."

The little child he last speaks of was baby Margaret, just born, a comfort, I think, to the [99] heart of the dear mother, greater even than the loving letters her husband wrote her.

But in London, Irving was not long allowed to keep his church. Many of those who had once held him so high did not like his message now, and they

Under the walls of the big prison he preached the gospel of his Master.

turned against him. He was cast out; but had said, "It is a small matter to be cast out of a house; it is a small matter this, seeing we have 'a house not made with hands, eternal in the heavens,' and are here but as pilgrims and sojourners on the earth, as all our fathers were. The Lord, we do not doubt, will provide us another, and if not, we are no worse off than He who was accustomed to preach the glad tidings of the kingdom by the Sea of Galilee; who taught His flock in the fields and desert places of Judea, and on the Mount of Olives. We can take ourselves to the fields and open places around this great city, and there I can feed my flock. We cannot be worse off than He who, to seek retirement, went up into a desert mountain to pray, and who had not where to lay His head; and when they all went to their several homes, He went to the Mount of Olives during the night to sleep there. We are not worse off than He. Oh, it is a small matter to be turned out of our church. He will soon recompense us with 'a city which hath foundations, whose builder and [100] maker is God.' The day is near at hand when the heavens shall be opened, and He, the Son of Man, shall appear in the clouds, with power and great glory, and when His saints shall be taken to Him, to dwell before His throne."

And for a time he and his faithful followers had no place for meeting large enough to take them all in. Then it was that Irving, as he had said, went out into the streets, to the vacant greens and the fields, and there in the summer days multitudes stood hushed before him, as on the parched city grass, or under the walls of the big prison, he preached the gospel of his Master Jesus who was soon to come, with an eloquence higher and stronger than when the greatest of the land had crowded to hear him in his church.

But not all heard him gladly. Every day there were many who insulted and threatened him, and sometimes, except for the protection of friends, he would have been beaten and perhaps killed. Some of his brethren were thrown into prison. It was a time, too, of excitement and terror among the people. Cholera was raging in the country, and many hearts were faint, failing them for fear. But Irving knew no fear; and when he felt a touch of the dread disease, he prayed for strength, and went to his preaching [102]twice that day, though weak and sick; and the next day felt himself healed and well.

The Albury Conferences continued for five years, and Henry Drummond especially was a faithful brother, and a tower of strength to Irving. Not only those who attended those conferences, but hundreds of others, were now proclaiming the coming of the Lord. Irving, however, had not a long life before him. He preached the message of Jesus' coming for about nine years; then in 1834, when the message in America was little more than started, Edward Irving was called to rest. He died, preaching almost to the last day, in the city where he had begun his ministry, Glasgow, Scotland. Thomas Carlyle, his friend but not his follower, wrote of him: "But for Irving I had never known what the communion of man with man means. His was the freest, brotherliest, bravest human soul mine ever came in contact with. I call him, on the whole, the best man I have ever, after trial enough, found in this world, or now hope to find." [104]

Wolff attended a great conference at Albury Park, where he learned the advent message

IX

MISSIONARY TO THE WORLD

"Hadji Wolff, you must not go to Abyssinia. There are great dangers in that, and you are like to lose your life." So spoke a Mohammedan ruler in Arabia to Joseph Wolff, missionary to the world, as he was planning an expedition into Africa.

But Wolff answered: "For a great object one may expect the assistance of God, in the time of danger. You expose your life among the wild Arabs, to bring them to order."

"Yes; but I am provided with arms."

"And so am I," said Wolff.

The sheik looked at him in astonishment. Wolff carried neither gun nor sword, nor had he any bodyguards or soldiers with him.

"With what kind of arms?" asked the ruler.

"With prayer, zeal for Christ, and confidence in His help," answered Wolff, "and also with the love of God and my neighbor in my heart; and my Bible in my hand."

Said the ruler, "I have no answer to that."

Joseph Wolff is called "the missionary to the world" because he traveled over so large a part [105] of it to carry the Christian faith and especially the message of Jesus' coming. He traveled in Europe, Asia, Africa, and North America; and like another Paul, in the course of his missions he encountered "perils of waters, perils of robbers, perils by mine own countrymen, perils by the heathen, perils in the city, perils in the wilderness, perils in the sea, perils among false brethren."

Born a Jewish lad in Bavaria, Germany, in 1796, young Wolff at the age of thirteen embraced the Christian faith and was cast out by his family. So young as this, he began a life of wandering, but always seeking knowledge, and [106] so studying in many schools, Catholic and Protestant, and becoming one of the most learned men of the times, with a knowledge of twenty-seven languages besides many dialects, and a noted scholar in the sacred literatures of Jews, Mohammedans, and Christians. But best of all, he was a devoted follower of the Lord Jesus Christ, for whose sake he endured many things and brought the knowledge of the Redeemer to peoples in lands around the earth.

In 1831, the year that William Miller began to preach, Joseph Wolff set out for a journey to Bokhara, in the heart of Asia. It was a very wild country, with a savage king, and the country between it and Persia, whence Wolff would start, was wilder still. Many travelers had been killed in those countries, and especially was a man in danger when he was known to be a Christian. Wolff reached Persia, and there began to prepare for his journey. Some native merchants, who traded in Bokhara, were asked how Wolff could go most safely.

Said Wolff, "I am provided with arms."

They replied, "He cannot go."

"Why not?" asked Wolff.

They answered, "They will kill you in Khorassan, because they cannot bear Christians. And if you should slip safely through Khorassan, and arrive in Sarakhs, where there are six [107] thousand tents of the Turkomans, they will keep you a slave. And if you were to slip through Sarakhs safely and arrive in Merv, you will still be in the same danger. And if you should slip safely through Merv, and arrive in Bokhara, you will either be kept there and never be allowed to leave, or killed, as they killed Morecroft and Guthrie and Trebeck six years ago."

But Wolff replied, "God is mighty above all things; he will take care of me."

He hired four camels and loaded them with goods, mostly Bibles, and set out with a caravan. Several times they were in danger from robbers. Sometimes they slept out on the desert sands, sometimes in the ruins of old castles, sometimes in cities.

When they were about half way to Bokhara, his companions came to him and said: "Hadji Wolff [hadji means holy man], we are now coming to a very dangerous city, the city of Burchund. They will never allow a Christian within its walls, but if they discover him they will put him to death. Yet we must pass through Burchund to go to Bokhara. So this is what we will do. We will time our march to come to the city just as the sun is going down, as they close the gates. We will slip within, and make ourselves very small, and we will stay at the inn until the stars [109] begin to pale in the sky. Then we will saddle up; and as soon as the gates are opened, we will go on our way. And so perhaps they will not know that a Christian has been within their walls."

So they did. They timed their march and came to the city just before the gates were shut. They slipped within and, as they said, they made themselves very small. They talked little, and tried to attract no notice. So they stayed all night, and in the morning, when the stars began to pale in the sky, they saddled up, went to the gates, and as soon as these were opened they rode on their way, believing that they had safely passed the dangerous city of Burchund. But not so! Though Wolff had kept in the background, though he was dressed as all the

"They will kill you in Khorassan, because they cannot bear Christians."

people of the land were dressed, and though he could speak their tongue, he could not be hid. You can never hide a Christian; for his manner and his voice are different from those of other men; they are like Jesus'. So someone suspected Wolff. And in the morning, after Wolff had gone, this suspicious person went to the ruler of the city, who was called the ameer, and said to him: "Do you know there was a Christian dog within the city of Burchund this night? He is on the way to Bokhara, and now he is gone, this Christian dog, unpunished." [110] When the ameer heard this, he called to him armed horsemen and commanded them to ride after Wolff, overtake him, and drag him back to be tried and condemned before him. The horsemen overtook him at the end of the day. They dragged him from his horse, and compelled him to walk all the way back to Burchund. When they arrived there, Wolff, bruised and worn, was given no rest. The ameer called his counsellors around him in his council chamber. They brought Wolff in and stood him before them. He might not sit in their presence; for only a guest might sit. They stood him up, and the ameer began to question him.

"What is your name?"

"It is Joseph Wolff."

"Where do you come from?"

"I come from the great kingdom of England."

"How far is that?"

"In a direct line, through Constantinople, and then by land, it is seven thousand miles; but as I have come, it is fifteen thousand miles."

"And where do you go?"

"I go to the kingdom and city of Bokhara."

"For what purpose?"

"I go to find my people, the Jews, and to carry to them the glorious message of a soon coming Saviour, even Jesus Christ the mighty, [111] who shall bring judgment to the good and to the evil, and restore all things in perfectness, as at the beginning."

Then the ameer, astonished that one should confess Christ when such a confession meant death, exclaimed in amazement, "You are a Christian, then?"

And Wolff replied, "I am an humble follower of the Lord Jesus Christ."

The ameer began to question him.

Still more amazed, the ameer asked, "Why do you mind what they believe in Bokhara? Why do you not stay at home with your family, eat, drink, and be merry?"

And Wolff replied, quoting first a Mohammedan poet: "Sadi says, 'The world, O brother, remains not to anyone. Fix therefore thy heart on the Creator of the world, and it shall be well with thee.' I have found out by the reading of this book [and he held out a Bible] that one can bind one's heart to God only by believing in Jesus; and believing this, I am like one who walks in a beautiful garden, and smells the odor of the roses and hears the warbling of the nightingales; and I do not like to be the only one so happy; therefore I go about in the world inviting others to walk with me arm in arm in that same beautiful garden."

When they heard him say this, all in the room rose as one man, they clapped their hands, and cried, "A holy man! A holy man! A dervish indeed!

Pioneer Stories

Drunk with the love of God! Sit down! Read to us from your book."

So, all at once, by the wisdom of the reply God gave him to make, Wolff's state was changed from that of a prisoner about to be condemned [113] to death as a "Christian dog," to that of an honored guest. "Sit down," they said; "read to us from your book."

And so Wolff opened his Bible to Isaiah and to the gospels, and read to them the prophecy and the story of Jesus: how He was born a babe in Bethlehem while the shepherds watched and the angels sang; how as He grew up He went about doing good and healing all that were oppressed of the devil; how wicked men took Him and slew Him upon the cross on Calvary, but God raised Him from the dead on the third day; how He ascended to heaven, where now He sits on the right hand of the throne of God, soon to come as a glorious King and bring His reward to the faithful and His judgment to the wicked. At last for weariness he could go on no longer.

Then they asked him, "Have you any more of those books?"

"Oh, yes," said Wolff, "I have many." He sent his servant down, who brought up armloads of books, and Wolff gave a Bible to every man in the room, the only men in the whole city, perhaps, who could read.

Then they said to him, "Hadji Wolff, you cannot leave us now. You must stay with us and teach us." So they took him in, and he lived while there in the house of the chief dervish. [114]

Every time he went out upon the street, he would find a crowd of men on this corner and on that, a dervish at the center of every crowd, reading to them from the Bible, the Christians' holy book, which before they would never touch. When they would see Wolff, they would call, "Hadji Wolff, come over and tell us what this means."

So for two whole weeks Wolff stayed with them and taught them. And when at last he said that he must go on his journey, they brought him in honor to the gate of their city, the ameer and all his chief men accompanying him, to bid him farewell. They loaded him with gifts, and as he departed they cried; "God go with you! Allah be with you, Hadji Wolff. You came to us, we thought, an enemy, but God has shown us that you are our friend; for you are a man who is drunk with the love of God!" [115]

X

CHILDREN IN SWEDEN

All over the world the advent message was being given. But I cannot tell you stories of it in every country, for it would make too big a book. Would you like to hear the story of how the children preached in Sweden? Over in that country the law let nobody preach except the priests of the state church, and *they* wouldn't give the message. So the Lord worked upon the hearts of some of the common people to tell Sweden that the Lord was coming. Now the priests did not like this, so they had these people arrested, and hindered the work all they could. Even some who were very young were persecuted. In one place, the county of Orebro, there were two young men, Ole Boquist, fifteen years old, and Erik Walbom, eighteen years old, who began to preach the coming of the Lord. They were not allowed to preach in the churches, so the people gathered to hear them in private houses, and oftentimes even out in the woods. The priest tried to stop this; he was going to have the young men arrested. But they fled to the woods and stayed out there, away from their [116] homes, for six weeks. Finally, however, they went to see the priest. He thought they must be crazy, and he felt of their pulses to see if they were sick. But when he found they were in good health, he grew angry, and had the police arrest them.

They were thrown into a dirty cell among thieves, and soon brought before the governor for examination. The governor stood them up [117] and lashed them with a prison whip until he grew weak, and then he had another man lash them again. Next they were examined by a doctor and he sent them to an insane asylum. Here they were taken to one side, and a large powerful stream

They fled to the woods.

of very cold water was turned on them. When they put up their hands to protect their heads, they were knocked down, and left there in the water until they found strength to get up, when they had to go through it all again. Then they were taken before the doctor, who said, as they stood shivering, "I see you are cold. I'll soon warm you up," and taking a large bundle of sticks, he beat them until he could no longer. Then they were sent back to their cells.

After some time spent in this asylum, or prison, they were let go. They had been treated so badly that they both fell sick and almost died. The Lord raised them up again, however, and they preached once more. This time, when the priests tried to have them arrested, the good King Oscar sent word that they were to be left alone, and so he protected them.

In other places where the older ones could not preach, the Lord did a most wonderful thing. Little children who could not read or write were moved upon

Children in Sweden

to tell of the coming of Jesus. In the humble cottages where they were born, they [118] began to repeat the very words of the Bible: "Fear God and give glory to Him, for the hour of His judgment is come." And then they would reprove the people for their sins and tell them to get ready for Jesus' coming. The people flocked out to hear them. Let us go in imagination with some of them to one of these meetings.

Soon the cottage comes in sight.

It is winter. There has not been much snow, but the lakes and the rivers and the marshes are all frozen over, and as we start out for the cottage, two miles away, where lives the [119] little girl we have heard of, we see people coming from every direction, across fields, over the frozen ground and water.
Soon the cottage comes in sight, snuggled down under the hill that protects it from the north winds. One-storied and low it is, with dead grass-blades peeping up through the scanty snow on its roof, and its dull red sides glow rather sullenly across the dreary landscape. Inside, however, all is cheer. The tall gray earthenware stove has been freshly fed, and inside its heavy timbered walls and under its turf roof, the large room glows with warmth and cheer.

Some few besides the family are there when we enter, and the eldest son, an earnest, fair- haired young man, is telling the group of how he was won from reckless ways by the warnings of his baby sister. Like an angel of God, he says, she seemed as she pointed out the end the ale- house was leading him to. "And how could she know, the pretty one, the little innocent," says Hans, "what evil men do in their drink? Surely the angels teach her, and leave her white as ever from the evil she describes."

"We know not," says the father, "what the spirit is, save it be the wonderful gift of God. For she says the hour of God's judgment is [120] come; and who was there to teach her that? But I have found her words in the Bible."

"It was not the priest," declares the mother, "for we have never heard the like from him, and we have never been to hear the advent heralds preach."

All this time the little girl of five is playing about the room, never noticing the talk that is so much about herself. Absorbed in her play with her brother, two years older (they are driving a reindeer sledge like the Lapps), she is as happy and childlike as any of her age. The older children, awed by the presence of the strangers, keep shyly in the background. It seems a strange meeting, where we have come to hear a preacher, and find the preacher playing reindeer sledge. And yet it is very solemn too; for the little child, now so innocent in her play, will soon be moved to speak as a messenger of God.

The room fills up, and many cannot get in, so they stand about the open door, willing to endure the cold if they can only hear. And when the murmur of voices at last is hushed, in expectation of what is coming, then the little girl looks up from her play, surveys the people [121] with grave eyes, and comes forward a little in the room.

"The spirit is upon her," whisper the people.

In her clear, childish voice she starts a hymn, and some of the people join in. At the close, her father lifts her to the table, and there she stands for a moment, and then opens her baby lips to proclaim: "Blow ye the trumpet in Zion, and sound an alarm in My holy mountain: let all the inhabitants of the land tremble: for the day of the Lord cometh, for it is nigh at hand."

The tall clock loudly ticks off its seconds in the silence that follows her first words. Then in solemn tones, with slow, graceful gestures learned on earth, she

She opens her baby lips to proclaim: "The day of the Lord cometh."

calls upon the backslidden and the worldly to turn again to their Saviour. Old men's heads are bowed, and the younger sit trembling, as she points out, with Scripture proof, the nearness of the judgment day. And as she tells of the love of Jesus, who will receive the lowest and the lowliest, sobs rise from every part of the room, and penitent sinners cry out for mercy.

The neighbors know the child. Dutiful and obedient she is to her parents, living herself so she may see Jesus; and they know the sage has entered her own young life. But this power,—it is, as they say, the angels who talk to her. Almost an angel herself she seems, and truly she is a messenger of God. The people remember how the older ones who preached this [123] message have been silenced in the jails; but God's message, they say, cannot be stopped. Out of the mouth of babes and sucklings hath God perfected praise.

As the little girl closes with a call for all to come to Jesus who have not already done so, an old man, a father in the neighborhood, but not a priest, kneels down to pray, and all fall upon their knees with him. He prays earnestly, and afterwards many others pray, some pleading for themselves, some for dear ones who are not yet saved.

The short afternoon is gone, and the shadows slip over the assembly as they still kneel. And when they rise, it is to sing another hymn for closing. The little girl has slipped down from the table, and sits meekly in a chair by her mother, quiet as any little girl by her mother's side, no longer the preacher. Her message has been given, her work is done for today; and they who would find peace turn to the old men and the old women, Christian fathers and mothers who can lead them to Jesus in private prayer and study.

At last we all slip out to go back over the frozen lakes, under the clear white moonlight, to our homes, made certain in our souls that the King is near the door. [124]

XI

CHILDREN IN AMERICA

Not only in Sweden and other countries of Europe, but here in America, God used the children to give the message. Not all of them stood up to preach, as did the children in Sweden, because here, you see, the older people could preach. But they all felt the need of getting ready to meet Jesus, and of helping others to do it. Is it not just as grand to help someone quietly, though nobody else knows it, as to help someone where everybody can see it? I'm sure it is. And if we are always thinking of helping somebody else, and not thinking about ourselves, why then the Lord will show us what to do and when to do it, whether it is teaching the commandments, or filling the woodbox, or speaking in meeting, or washing the dishes, or maybe sometime preaching when there is nobody else to do it. But you may be sure that any one who is thinking about himself and what people say of him and what they ought to do for him, will never be able to do God's work.

It was hard for children, as well as for anybody else, to stand for the truth then. When [125] they went to school, oftentimes they were hooted at, and shoved and abused, and called all sorts of names; but they had learned to be gentle and not to say anything bad in reply. Sometimes men who were evil tried to take the children away from their parents and keep them so they would forget Jesus and His coming. They would claim that the fathers and mothers were crazy and not able to take care of their children, and they would get orders from the judge to take the children away. You know in our own times, before the end comes, men will do this to some of the children. Will you be ready for that?

Pioneer Stories

One time, over near Oswego, New York, there lived out in the country a mother who believed in the coming of Jesus, and who had taught her children to believe in it too. A boy whom I told you one story, Irving Guilford, was sitting in the house one day with this mother and her children. He had been fasting for nine days. As they sat there, this boy had a sort of vision.

"There is somebody coming from the village to get your children," said he to the mother. "There are two men with a warrant."

And pretty soon, as they sat watching in dread, they saw the two men coming down the road. [126]

"Oh, what shall we do?" cried the poor mother.

"Let us pray," said Irving Guilford; and they all knelt down and prayed that God, in this time of trouble, would help them, and not let the [127] children be taken away by wicked men. They all felt assured that the Lord would protect them; and just then the men rapped at the door.

The mother opened it, and the men started to come in; but they could not. They backed away from the door, stood looking at the mother a moment, and then, without a word, they turned and walked away. They said afterwards there was an influence that met them at the open door which they could not stand against. The Lord drove them and the children were saved.

Not always were the parents helpers, though. Sometimes children believed when their parents didn't. And often this made it very hard for the children. In one place, at West Gardiner, Maine, there were ten or twelve children who believed in the message, and now wanted to be baptized. But some of the older people in the church laughed at them, and told them they weren't old enough to be baptized, that they didn't know what it meant. But they had been listening with their ears open, and their hearts too, and they did know that baptism is meant to show that our old selves are dead and buried, and we rise with the new life that Jesus gives, to live afterwards as Jesus lived. And they would not give up the thought of being baptized. Then some of the people threatened them, and tried to [128] frighten them, but those dear children, some of whom were only seven years old, and some of whom were as old as fifteen, would not be frightened. They knew it was joy to confess Jesus, and that He was as ready to save and bless children as when He was here on earth.

Children in America

They backed away from the door.

At last their parents sent word to James White to come and baptize them. Still their enemies tried to stop them. They laughed loudly and scornfully. "What does Mr. White think these babies can tell of their experience?" they asked.

But James White loved those children, and he determined he would not let their enemies triumph over them. So he called the people together to the schoolhouse with the children, and he told them he would not be so cruel as to make little children stand up alone and tell of their experience before those who opposed them. He called the children forward to the front seat, and after

In a beautiful little lake near by the children were baptized.

he had talked, in a short sermon, about baptism and what it means, he asked the children some questions, just as though they were his class in school, and he their teacher. And they stood up one by one and answered the questions, and told how they loved Jesus, and how He had forgiven their sins. Many of the people wept. Then they all went to a beautiful [129] little lake near by, and there the children were buried in baptism by the young minister. They had triumphed, and though of course they had many hard things to meet afterwards, Jesus was very precious to them.

"I love Jesus; I love my parasol."

The children felt they had work to do in those days. As I told you before, they used to have little prayer meetings among themselves, where they would pray for one another, and for those who were not converted. It was not just a happy feeling they prayed for. That does not always come even when we do right. But they prayed to know right from wrong. And the Lord answered them.

All through the land, the children were working for others, for their playmates and for older people. They prayed for them and led them to pray, and many were converted. But most of all, the children who prayed also worked. If a boy or girl were lazy or disobedient to parents, or loud and rough, do you think their prayers would do very much? I'm sure they wouldn't. And so the real workers were faithful in doing their chores and housework, and in running errands, and in speaking gently and acting modestly. They were real boys and girls, who could run and shout and climb, but they were not rough. And they were ready to give up their own [131] ways and their choicest treasures, if it could help spread the news Jesus' coming.

There was a little girl at one of the camp meetings in Buckston, Maine, a little girl about six years old. She had learned to love Jesus and to look for His coming. Her greatest treasure was a little pink parasol which had been given her for a present. She loved that parasol so much she used to carry it around all the time, whether the sun was shining or not. She even would take it to bed with her. But she heard that we must give up everything for Jesus, if we would get ready for His coming. [132]

"Oh, dear," she thought, "must I give up my parasol?" One day she sat with her mother in the tent during the meeting, thinking, "I love Jesus; I love my parasol. I love Jesus; I love my parasol. Can I give up my parasol for Jesus?" She grasped it tightly in her arms, looking at it lovingly, and her face went red and white by turns. At last she burst into tears, and cried out loud, "Dear Jesus, I want to love Thee and go to heaven! Take away my sins. I give myself to Thee, parasol and all." And then she threw her arms around her mother, saying, "Oh mother, I'm so happy, for Jesus loves me, and I love Him better than my parasol or anything else."

All the people in the tent rejoiced with her, for they knew it was just as hard for her to give up her parasol as it would be for them to give up their houses and lands. Then the little girl was told that since she was willing to let the parasol go, and it didn't stand between her and Jesus, she might keep it, for it would no longer keep her away from Jesus.

Among those who watched this little girl's devotion was another girl, a very sad girl, whose heart was warmed and helped by the little child's deed of sacrifice. This girl's name was Ellen Harmon. Five years before, she had had a [133] terrible accident. An angry schoolmate had thrown a stone at her and her sister, as they were hurrying away home; and as Ellen turned to look, the stone struck her on the nose, and she fell unconscious. She was taken borne, and for three weeks she lay still and white, knowing nothing of what happened. When she awoke, it was to find that the accident had greatly changed the features of her face, so that even her father, when he came home some weeks afterwards, did not know her.

She was sick and weak a long time, and everyone but her mother believed she would die. When she was able to be up, she found that she could not make her mind study, and her hand trembled so she could not write. Her old playmates shunned her, too, for she looked so very different from the strong and pretty little girl they had known.

Ellen was timid, and the way many treated her made her shrink more and more from being with people or talking with them. But during her sickness she learned how Jesus loved her, and for awhile she was very happy. Then as she saw how she must go through life always feeble and sick, and how she could not study so as to get a good education, as she wished, and how people shunned her, or worse still, pitied her, she [134] felt very bad, and finally she lost the feeling that Jesus loved her. Then she used often to lie awake at night, trembling and crying, sometimes kneeling down while her sister slept, to pray for hours at a time.

So now at this camp meeting she felt very sad. But when she saw what the little girl did, and when she had heard what the ministers were telling the people of how to come to Jesus, she found comfort, and once more the peace of God came to her, and she was happy. The world seemed all new again, the birds and the bees sang praise to Jesus, and the flowers smiled up into His face. As they were driving home, they passed through the streets of their home town, in the midst of workingmen who were talking about common things. But Ellen's ears were tuned to catch only praise, and she thought they were all talking about Jesus, too.

"Why, mother," she said, "these men are all praising God, and *they* haven't been to the camp meeting."

The tears came into mother's eyes as she smiled, thinking of how it had seemed to her much the same when she was first converted.

Ellen was baptized, and joined the Methodist church. Her conscience was very tender, and she often felt that she was too wicked to have God [135] love her. So we all are—aren't we?—too wicked to deserve God's love; and yet He

Pioneer Stories

"Why, mother, these men are all praising God."

does love us. She read in the Sunday-school books of children who always did just right, and she thought, "I can never be as perfect as they were." Of course; for such children never lived. We all do wrong things. But if, because we love Jesus, we want to do right, He will forgive us when we ask Him to, and make us able to do right more and more. When we do right, it shows other people what Jesus is like, and makes them love Him. God does not give us eternal life in the new [136] earth because we do right, but we do right when He has saved us and Jesus lives in us. And we must come to be perfect before the end.

Ellen grew discouraged again. She believed Jesus was coming in 1844, but she did not see how she could be ready to meet Him. She was very frail and weak and timid. She felt she ought to speak in class-meeting, but she couldn't find courage. And then, knowing she had neglected her duty, she went into despair. But Jesus loved her, and as He saw her bowed down with sorrow, He came to her to comfort her.

One night she had a dream, in which she saw people going into a beautiful temple. Those who would go in, she understood, would be saved when time should close, but all others would be lost. Many were making fun of those who entered, and were pulling them away. At last she pressed her way in, where she saw a bleeding lamb, who represented Jesus. Upon high seats many people were already seated, singing songs of gladness that they were saved. As she pressed forward to get near the lamb, suddenly a trumpet sounded, the building shook, the people cried out in gladness; and then—all was dark, and she awoke to find herself in the silent night, alone.

This dream made her afraid she was lost. But soon she had another, in which a bright [137] angel came to her and said, "Do you wish to see Jesus? He is here, and you may see Him. Take all you have, and follow me." So with her little trinkets all gathered up in her arms, she followed him up a long, frail stairway. It was a dizzy place, and the angel told her to keep her eyes fixed upward, lest she fall. Many were falling. At last, at the top, the angel bade her leave her treasures, and then they entered a building, and she came into the presence of Jesus. He smiled upon her as He had upon the children He blessed in Galilee; and laying His hand upon her head, He said, "Fear not." He showed her many beautiful things, too wonderful to describe, and at last she dreamed that she was taken back to earth again; and she awoke. But now she felt sure that Jesus loved her. Now she told her mother all her troubles, and her mother comforted her, and then sent her to a minister named Stockman. And just as Eli, long time ago, saw that God had been talking with Samuel, so this minister saw that Jesus was working with Ellen; and he said to her, as his eyes filled with tears, "Ellen, you are only a child, but you have had a wonderful experience. Jesus must be preparing you for some special work."

And Ellen went to work. Not only did she, in the Methodist class-meeting and other places, [138] tell of her experience, and how happy she was in preparing to meet Jesus at His soon coming, but she worked with her young friends, gathering them into little meetings for prayer and study. Some of her friends were older, too, a few even married persons. Some were giddy and thoughtless, and they thought it queer for Ellen to work [139] for them. But not discouraged, she prayed earnestly for them, and at last they all, except one, were converted to God, and began to study and work for Jesus, too.

You would think that the church people would be glad to have her do this work. But some of them hated to hear that Jesus was coming, and they said

Ellen was too zealous. Nevertheless, she did not lose heart, but went on in her life of prayer and love and helpfulness; and, as you shall see later, the Lord was preparing her for a great and wonderful work. [140]

Ellen studied with her young friends.

XII

THE MIDNIGHT CRY

Going to Exeter camp meeting? Yes, thousands on the way. Wagons, stagecoaches, railroad trains, and steamboats were loaded with people, going to Exeter camp meeting. Exeter is in New Hampshire, at the head of a long arm of Great Bay, near the ocean. It was only a short distance from the states of Maine and Massachusetts, and from all three of these states the people poured in. Even some from New York and farther away attended.

It was in the late summer of 1844. The believers in the coming of Jesus had during this year had more and more opposition in the churches, and very generally they had been cast out or had felt it wise to withdraw. And because they believed in the near coming, or advent, of Jesus, they began to be called Adventists, though as yet they had organized no church, but simply met in companies.

There had been a great disappointment. The Adventist people had looked for the Lord to come in the spring. Why? Well, you remember that the 2300 days, or years, at the end [141] of which the sanctuary was to be cleansed, began in 457 B.C. Twenty-three hundred years from that time comes to the end of the year 1843; only, since the Jewish year begins, not on January 1, but on March 21, the end of the Jewish year 1843 came on March 20, 1844. And they all thought Jesus would come then. But He did not come, and now it was the middle of August.

"Going to Exeter camp meeting?"

"Yes, neighbor; come along. I think we'll get new light there."

"What light?"

"Why, light on the tarrying time. Haven't you heard we're in the tarrying time? Well, come along to Exeter."

And there the great camp lay spread out, hundreds of tents, many small, some of them large, housing a whole church.

Joseph Bates started from his home away down in Fairhaven, Massachusetts, to go to Exeter. As be traveled on the cars, every once in a while would come to his mind an impression, as though an angel pressed it down: "You are going to have new light here, something that will make the work go with great speed."

He reached the campground, and it was not long until he set out to find the new light. Oh, [142] but you must think how bitterly disappointed the people had been. The prophecy had seemed to fail. Jesus had not come. What could they say to those who scoffed? Yet some there were who believed so thoroughly that Jesus' coming was near, that this spring they had not put in any crops. They thought there would never be another winter. And others, when July came, went out to cut their hay but felt so strongly that Jesus was coming that they left the field and did not gather their crops. There would be no winter in which to need them, they reasoned, and so left them.

So Joseph Bates passed on from tent to tent, stopping at each and asking, "Do you know of any new light on the subject?"

"New light?" said one man he asked. "Come to the Exeter tent. They have new light there."

So to the Exeter tent they went; and seated there, they heard what was called, "The Midnight Cry."

Surely you remember the midnight cry. In a story Jesus told to His disciples, there were ten maidens waiting to meet the bridegroom when he should come. But he tarried and tarried, and they grew weary, and they all fell asleep. Then at midnight arose the cry, "Behold, the bridegroom cometh. Go ye out to meet him." And [143] they all rose up to get ready. That story was made for just this time.

At the Exeter tent they were telling about it. The Adventist people, they said, had been like the maidens who were expecting the bridegroom, Christ.

*"Come to the Exeter tent.
They have new light there."*

Pioneer Stories

But He did not come in the spring, as they expected Him to. So now they had all been in the "tarrying time," and they had all been asleep. That is, they did not know when to look for Him, and thought perhaps He would never come, and so they began to plan for life on this earth again. Thus they had been asleep. But now they had found the definite time of His coming. How was that? And Joseph Bates, who was a very exact man, and always wanted proof for everything, sat listening very intently now.

How was that? Why, said the speaker, the sanctuary was to be cleansed after 2300 years, beginning with the going forth of the decree to restore and build Jerusalem. (Daniel 8:14; 9:25.) That decree was made by Artaxerxes, king of Persia, in 457 B.C., and 2300 years brings us down to A.D. 1843. Now if Artaxerxes made the decree to build Jerusalem the very first day of the Jewish year 457 B.C., then the 2300 years would end the last day of the Jewish year, 1843, or the 20th day of March, 1844. But, said the speaker, Artaxexes did not make the decree on [145] the first day of that year, but several months later, away along in the fall, so that 2300 years from that time would not end until the fall of 1844.

"On just what day, do you ask?" he said. "Here we come to another thing we have overlooked. The prophecy says the sanctuary is to be cleansed at the end of the 2300 years. Well, in the service of the tabernacle or temple among the Jews (which was called the sanctuary), the Day of Atonement, when the sanctuary was cleansed every year, came on the tenth day of the seventh Jewish month." They were getting much nearer to the truth about the sanctuary than they knew, but they did not see it yet. They still thought the sanctuary was this earth.

"Well," he went on,—and he reckoned it all out before them,—" the tenth day of the Jewish seventh month falls this year on October 22. That is therefore the day of atonement, when the sanctuary will be cleansed. And therefore, on that day, the twenty-second of October, 1844, Jesus will come."

Joseph Bates heaved a long sigh of satisfaction. It was as clear as day. And so it is to us, only we know now that the sanctuary is not this earth, and that therefore the cleansing of the sanctuary did not mean the coming of Jesus. [146] But on that day, October 22, 1844, Jesus entered upon His work of cleansing the sanctuary. And what that means we shall find out before we have finished this book.

"This is the call," said the speaker, "that goes out at midnight: 'Behold, the Bridegroom cometh; go ye out to meet Him!' We have all been asleep, brethren; let us awake and trim our lamps, that we may be ready when the Bridegroom comes."

"Amen! Amen!" said deep voices. And from back in the tent rose the beginning of a song:

> "We will all go out to meet Him
> When He comes, when He comes....
>
> Behold, He cometh! Behold, He cometh!
> Be robed and ready, for the Bridegroom comes."

Thus began the midnight cry. One minister, S. S. Snow, had believed for several months that the time the Lord would come was October 22, 1844.

From back in the tent rose the beginning of a song.

Pioneer Stories

The year before this, William Miller had called attention to the tenth day of the seventh month as something very important, but he did not know just what. Now, when Snow had been preaching this midnight cry, Miller, Himes, and other leading men, were very slow in taking it up. [147] They hardly thought it was true. But at the Exeter camp meeting the message came with such power that none could resist it, and soon Himes, Miller, and all the other ministers believed it and began to preach it.

When Bates returned from the Exeter camp meeting to his home, another minister, named Macomber, went with him. The brethren at home at first could scarcely believe the midnight [148] cry was right. The next Sunday after reaching home, Bates and Macomber attended the Adventist meeting in New Bedford, two miles away. R. Hutchinson, from Canada, was preaching. But it seemed he could not say anything; he was confused. And at last he sat down, saying, "I can't preach."

Macomber was sitting on the platform with him. He rose, much excited, remembering what had been told at the Exeter camp meeting. "Oh," he exclaimed, "I wish I could tell you what I have seen and heard, but I cannot," and he sat down, too.

Then Joseph Bates rose from his seat in the room, saying, "I can." And with words flowing as easily as water down a watercourse, he told of the new light of the midnight cry. The Lord gave him special help in making the people see. When he had finished, a sister came across the room, and said, "Brother Bates, I want you to preach that same good news to us this after noon."

Hutchinson now rose, and said, "If what Brother Bates says is true, I don't wonder that my preaching sounded like carpenter's chips."

Bates preached to them that evening, and when the sermon closed, the people rose in groups to speak, rejoicing that the Lord had given them the new light; and the cry went out, [149] "Behold, the Bridegroom cometh. Go ye out to meet Him!"

Fast and far the midnight cry sounded over the land. A paper called *The Midnight Cry* was quickly started, and it was scattered everywhere, telling of the mistake in reckoning which had been made, how it had been found out, and showing that the cleansing of the sanctuary was to begin on October 22,

The Midnight Cry

1844. It called attention to the parable of the ten virgins, the story that Jesus told for just this time. And don't you suppose they were glad to see how Jesus had thought of them down through so many years, and had told this story to encourage them here?

Everywhere the midnight cry was received, the people showed by their lives that they were truly getting ready for Christ. They searched their lives to find what faults they had, they prayed much, and all sought to be ready for Jesus when He should come. Those who truly believed showed by what they did that they believed. Some professed to believe, but did not really, and they showed this by what they did.

One man who said he believed Jesus was coming October 22, had a drove of hogs at just the right age for keeping over for the spring market. A stockman went to him to buy the hogs.

"No," said the man, "I don't think I'll sell [150] them now." And the stockman went away and told his people, "That man doesn't believe what he says he does."

"Why, how do you know?" they asked.

"Because," the stockman answered, "he says he believes the world is coming to an end this fall, and yet he doesn't want to sell his hogs until spring. He needn't talk to me; he doesn't believe a word of it."

But they who did believe showed it by what they did. They left their crops ungathered, their winter apples on the trees, their potatoes in the ground. And that did more preaching than any words they might have said.

Soon it came close down to the day of October 22. And over all the country the Adventist ministers ceased preaching, the believers gathered together, the work stopped, and all waited for the great day. And in that little time of waiting, when there was no more work to be done, there came men who had waked up too late. They had loved their money so much that they would not give it before. But now they felt sure the Lord was coming, and they brought their money in. Into the offices of the Adventist papers they came, and laid thousands of dollars before the editors. "Take it for the work," they begged. [151]

"We can't now," they answered, "we don't need it. We have hired printing presses to run day and night, and we have paid them advance: we don't want

Pioneer Stories

any more money."

"Then," the men urged, "take it and give it to the poor."

"No," said they, "we have provided for all the poor we can reach until the great day. We can't use your money."

And the men, the selfish men who had held on to their money until too late, turned away in anguish, saying, "It is too late! It is too late! God will not take our money now."

Were they not like the foolish maidens in the parable, whose lamps had gone out? So will it be in the very last time. And some will come up too late to the door; for the Bridegroom will say, "I know you not," and there will be weeping and gnashing of teeth. [153]

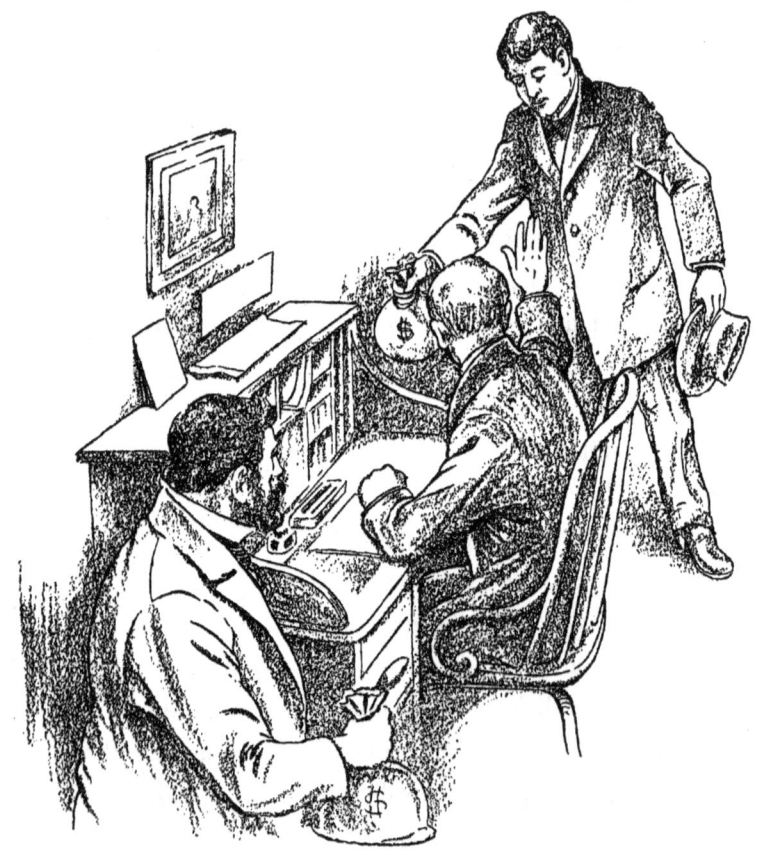

"Too late for money! We don't need it."

XIII

THE DISAPPOINTMENT

The last day! What a sound it has. No doubt, children, you have used that phrase many times, and it always meant a great deal to you. Perhaps it was the last day of school, and you looked out on the sunny fields and the deep, cool woods or the river, and you twitched in your seat for joy at the thought of the free days coming. Perhaps it was the last day of vacation, and you braced your mind, after its long rest from books, to take up a new year of study, and you rejoiced at the thought that you would be further along by the end of another year.

The last day! How you turned to take a last look at the familiar things: the teacher's desk, with its books and its globe and its strings of beads; the cabinet on the north wall, filled with insects and rocks and polished woods; and the peg where your cap always hung. Or else, that autumn day, the orchard playhouse under the apple tree, or the swimming hole by the tall old elms, the wild strawberry glades and the clumps of wild plum, with fruit long ago gone, but still sweet in memory. And in whichever place you [154] were, you said with a sigh half of gladness, half of regret, "It's the last day."

But can you think what the last day meant in that long ago time, to the people who said, as they watched the sun go down: "Tomorrow is the last day. We shall never see the sun set red again. Nor shall we have to hear the curses of the drunken and the scoffing tomorrow night. We have eaten our last supper on earth; the next we shall take with Jesus and the millions of the saved, in the light of the New Jerusalem. Tomorrow will see those blue skies rent, and our Saviour coming in glory. Tomorrow will stop the mocking mouth. Tomorrow will see the earth heaved up, mountains sinking, the ground opening, the sea rushing in, the cities in ruins, the earth reeling. Tomorrow we shall see Jesus. It is the last day"?

And as the farm boy did the milking, he thought, "This is the last time." As the ditch-digger put up his spade, he said, "I have no more use for you." As the merchant shut the door of his shop, he said, "This is the last time I shall turn the key."

And they had to think, "There's my neighbor who does not believe Jesus is coming. I shall never see him after tomorrow. But I have done my duty in warning him. And there might be [155] Aunt Eliza, and Uncle John; there might be Cousin Amy, and Phil, and little Josie. Oh, why would they not hear?" And the tears fell fast.

As the farm boy did the milking, he thought, "This is the last time."

"Tomorrow is the last day. And we shall see Abraham and Moses and Elijah in the kingdom of heaven. And we shall see Jesus. We shall walk on the streets of gold. We shall soon see the beautiful green fields of earth restored as in Eden. No more of this fair earth, this dark earth. Tomorrow is the last day."

And the sun came up that twenty-second day of October, 1844. The children were all up, with [156] their fathers and mothers; for who could tell

The Disappointment

whether the coming should be at dawn or at evening? And the house was swept, and the furniture in order. There was nothing to do but wait.

Where there were a number of Adventists together, they gathered in their meetinghouse, or sometimes out in the country, in the woods. When they were alone, they stayed in their houses; for they feared to go out where the unbelievers could find them.

And those unbelievers trembled. For all they shouted and made merry, yet in their hearts they trembled; for they said, "Suppose it should be! *Suppose* it should be!" But toward the trusting ones they acted angrily. If they met one, they pushed and jostled and jeered at him. And in some places the wicked gathered in companies to mock and make fun of those who looked for Jesus. What shrieks of terror they would have sent up had the dreadful event they mocked at come upon them!

The sun mounted higher and higher in the sky; but still the faithful watched. They watched and prayed. Sometimes, softly, they sang an advent hymn. For the last time they confessed their sins against one another. Their hearts must be made pure. [157]

But they were not left quietly alone. In some places mobs gathered around their places of worship, and mocked them, calling out to them, as the wicked children of Bethel had to Elisha,

"Go up! Go up! Why don't you go up?" And they sang rude songs, and pounded on the houses with clubs and stones.

The Adventist believers made their ears deaf to all these things. What did it matter, they thought: it would be only a little while, a few hours at the most, when all this would be changed; those who mocked now would shriek with terror when they should see the King, sitting upon the great white cloud, come to judge the world. And they looked longingly through the windows for the sign of His coming.

The sun passed the noon, it kept evenly on its way down, down the sky. At last it neared the horizon. Yet still there was time. The day was not quite gone. Jesus would yet come: He would not disappoint His people. So all over the land this cry of their hope went up from the hearts of men, women, and children who were looking for Jesus.

Pioneer Stories

But slowly, slowly, the sun went down. Its lower rim touched the hills, and quickly it sank out of sight. The day was gone, the great tenth day of the seventh month. Jesus had not come. [158] Into one another's blank faces brethren and sisters looked. The children clung to the hands of father and mother. No one could speak a word; no one could explain. Silently, with hearts crushed within them, they slipped out of doors, and by dark ways, to keep out of sight of the mob, they went sadly to their homes. They groped their way into the dark rooms, they felt around to find their seats; they dared not light their lamps. Outside somewhere the roughs of the town would be celebrating the failure, drinking, singing, joking. [159]

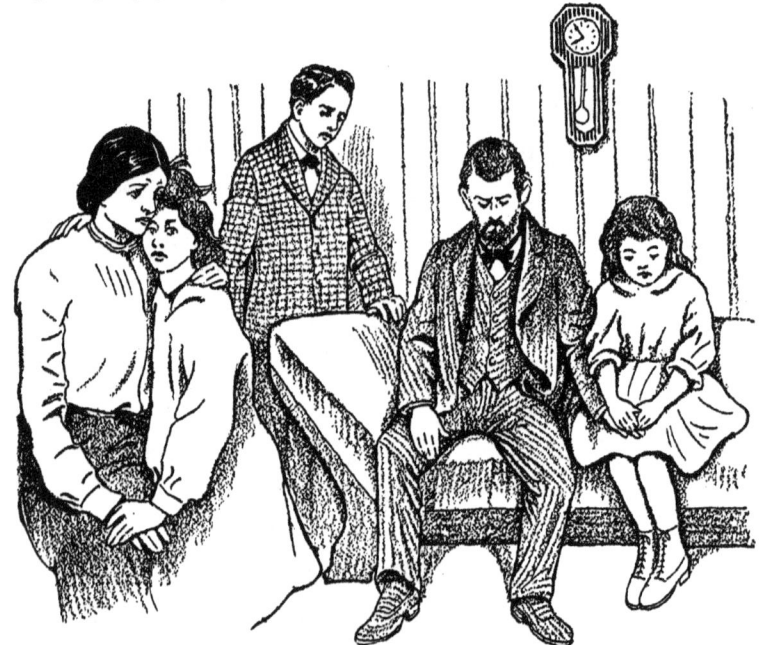

They sat silent, choking back their grief.

And the fathers and the mothers gathered their children within their arms, and sat silent, choking back their grief.

"Why didn't He come, father?" How the words of the little child struck into the heart! "We can't tell, my children. We shall have to wait, wait and see." And spent with grief, they slept.

Jesus did not fail. That day, October 22, 1844, was the tenth day of the seventh month, and on that day, according to prophecy, Jesus began to cleanse the sanctuary. Great things were going on in heaven that day, for the great High Priest, Jesus, was being escorted by angels into the holiest place of the sanctuary. And there, on that day, He began His work, which is still going on, and now almost finished.

And He did not forget His waiting people on earth. Though they were disappointed, cast down, though they knew not what to think, that night Jesus looked down with great love upon them, and strong angels were sent to watch over them and keep them; and if they would be patient, they should soon see what mistake they had made, they should understand in what glorious work they had been engaged, and from their disappointment they should gain new courage. [160]

It is a day to be remembered, October 22, 1844. On that day Jesus began the closing work which you and I know is now almost finished. And when He has finished it, He will quickly come to earth, even as the tried and faithful ones then looked to see Him come. Then He will reap the harvest of the earth.

Is it not a good day for us to remember? Can we not, on that day, have a great festival? Our harvests have been gathered in, and then we may thank the Lord for them. Jesus' harvest will soon be gathered in; and children, may you and I be gathered in that harvest. So on this day we may rejoice at what we have and what is promised, recounting the stories of what has happened to God's people since this message began, and looking forward to the time when it shall all be finished. [161]

"Till He come,"—O let the words
Linger on the trembling chords;
Let the "little while" between
In their golden light be seen;
Let us think how heaven and home
Lie beyond that—"Till He come."
—*Bickersteth.*

PART TWO

The dawn is breaking o'er us.
Look up, ye Sons of night!
There stretches on before us
Eternal day's delight.
Oh lift your trouble-burdened eyes,
To meet the promise of the skies.

The dawn is breaking o'er us.
Eternal morn is near.
The night that long outwore us
Shrinks back in mortal fear.
O Earth, farewell! Our spirit flies
To greet our kingdom in the skies.

Hiram Edson felt as it were a hand upon him.

XIV

LIGHT ON THE SANCTUARY

Over in the western part of New York, on the Erie Canal, there lies the snug little town of Port Gibson. In 1844 there was here a small company who believed Jesus would come on the tenth day of the seventh month; that is, October 22. Led by Hiram Edson, they gathered together to pray and to wait. But, just as everywhere else, the day passed slowly by, the sun sank, and they were left alone: Jesus had not come.

Ah! What a time of sadness! Men and women all cried; it seemed they could not pray. Worse it was to them than if they had lost father, mother, all brothers and sisters, and every friend. The night drew on, and some quietly slipped away to their homes. The others stayed, scarcely noticing their going, and still they wept and grieved, until at last the dawn of a new day came. And its grayness seemed the grayness of their lives. Was there, then, they reasoned to themselves, to be no second coming of Christ? Was the Bible all false? Was there no Jesus who had died for them? Should they never see that golden-home city of the redeemed, nor walk in [167] that country whose inhabitants should say, "I am no more sick"? Could there be no God at all?

"Not so, brethren," said Hiram Edson to the few who remained; "I remember how many times the Lord has sent us help and light when we needed it. There is a God, and He will hear us. Let us go and seek Him for light on this matter."

And so the brethren went out of the house in the gray dawn, back to the barn, and opening the granary they went in, closed the door, and kneeled down to pray. I cannot tell you what they said, nor how they were comforted; but of this I am sure, that they knew their prayers were heard and accepted in heaven where Jesus was, and they were promised they should know what their disappointment meant.

After breakfast, Edson said to one of his friends who was still with him, "Let us go over to see some of the brethren and comfort them." So they started across-lots, these two, going through a cornfield, where the corn had been cut, and stood in shocks. They were both thinking very deeply, and each walked without thinking of the other.

They came to the middle of the field, and suddenly Hiram Edson felt as it were a hand upon him, stopping him where he was. It seemed [168] as though a glory shone around him, and looking as in a vision he saw that Jesus, our High Priest, had entered that day into the Most Holy Place of the sanctuary in heaven, and there He would stay until He had finished the work of cleansing it.

The other man had gone on, not noticing that Edson had stopped. Now, coming to himself at the fence on the other side of the field, he paused, and looked around for his companion, and there he saw him away back in the middle of the field.

"Brother Edson," he called, "what are you stopping for?"

And Edson called back, "He is answering our morning prayer."

Then, coming up, Edson began telling him what he had seen and heard. "My mind," he said, "is carried to the tenth and eleventh chapters of Revelation, where John was told to take a little book from the angel's hand and eat it. It tasted like honey in the mouth, but when he had eaten it, it was as bitter as gall. That is our experience, brother," said Hiram Edson. "We have taken the book of the prophecies. Was it not sweet when we took it, to know that Jesus was coming yesterday? But now it is bitter, very bitter. Yet He says we must prophesy again before many people and nations [169] and tongues. And the sanctuary, I saw, is in heaven, and Jesus yesterday entered upon His work of cleansing it."

It seemed very new and strange to them both, but they believed, though they could not understand, and then they went on to tell the brethren.

Among Edson's friends was a Doctor Hahn, who lived at Canandaigua, on Lake Canandaigua, twelve miles away. He and his wife were believers in Jesus' coming. There was also a young man by the name of O. R. L. Crosier,

Edson, Hahn and Crosier studied together.

who lived sometimes with Doctor Hahn and sometimes [171] with Mr. Edson. He was a talented young man, and had helped in the spreading of the second advent message.

These three had been publishing a paper called *The Day Dawn*, to help give the warning. They could not put it out every week, for they were poor, but as often as they could get enough money, they would hire the printing office at Canandaigua to print a number of *The Day Dawn*.

Edson made a visit to Hahn and Crosier, and told them what had been revealed to him in regard to the sanctuary.

"Will the Bible bear that out?" asked Crosier.

"I believe it will, for I am sure it is the truth," said Edson.

Then Crosier began to study to see what he could find about the sanctuary question. And this is what he found:
1. "Sanctuary" means a sacred place, where God dwells.
2. The earth is never in the Bible called the sanctuary.
3. The tabernacle made by the Israelites in the wilderness, was called the

sanctuary, and afterwards the temple built in Jerusalem was also called the sanctuary. [171]

The tabernacle was called the sanctuary.

4. There were two rooms in this sanctuary, the first called the Holy Place, the second the Most Holy Place. In the Most Holy Place was the sacred ark, which held the law of God, the Ten Commandments, and upon its cover, called the mercy seat, there dwelt always a bright light, which was the presence of God Himself.

5. Into this Most Holy Place of the sanctuary the high priest went only once every year. He went in on the tenth day of the seventh month, and that day was called *the day of atonement*. The high priest went in before the ark, where God dwelt. He swung before him a censer filled with burning incense. There he stayed for some time, while the people outside all waited, breathless, listening to hear the tinkle of the little bells upon his robe when he should come out. They did not know but that for their sins God would slay their high priest. But he always came out, [172] bearing upon him the sins of the people. All the year long, the people had confessed their sins here at the sanctuary, slaying a lamb or some other animal at the same time, and the priest sprinkled some of its blood in the sanctuary. This was said to carry the people's sins into the sanctuary, and on this day of atonement the high priest was said to *cleanse the sanctuary*, by taking away the sins of the people.

At the door of the tabernacle, or temple, a goat was brought to the high priest, and laying his hands upon the goat's head, he confessed over him the sins

Light on theSanctuary

of the people, and then the goat was sent away to wander in the wilderness.

6. The high priest stood for Christ, who is our High Priest. The lamb which the sinner slew also stood for Christ, who was slain for our sins. The goat stood for Satan, who will have to bear all the sins that are forgiven, and be punished for them. And the sanctuary on earth was made after the pattern of one in heaven, so it stood for that sanctuary.
7. Therefore, there is a sanctuary in heaven, where Christ acts as our High Priest. At the end of the 2300 days He goes in to cleanse the sanctuary from all the sins of His people since the world began; and when He has finished cleansing the sanctuary, He will come out to His [173] waiting people. All their sins are taken away, and He will lay these sins on Satan, who will have to die for them. And then Jesus will take His people home.

From the prophecy of Daniel 8:14 we know that the cleansing of the sanctuary was to begin in 1844, and on the twenty-second day of October. So on that day, instead of coming to earth, Jesus began to cleanse the sanctuary in heaven, and in that sanctuary He is now. When He has finished its cleansing, He will come to receive His people. We are the people watching in the court, listening to hear His coming step. We cannot tell how long it will be, but we know it cannot be long.

All this Crosier found from studying the Bible. "That agrees," he said, "with what Brother Edson saw and heard. The sanctuary is in heaven."

This was talked over by all the brethren, and especially by Edson, Hahn, and Crosier. Said the first two to Crosier, "We must get out an other number of *The Day Dawn*, and tell this to the believers everywhere."

Their friends there near them were glad to hear this truth, for it explained their disappointment, and showed that Jesus had not left them, and they might expect Him to come very soon. [174]

So they agreed that if they could get money, they would send out this truth in *The Day Dawn*. And they worked and worked, and secured enough money at last, and oh, how glad they were to see the paper when it came from the printing

Over a year had passed by since Brother Edson saw that truth; for you see it had taken Brother Crosier and the others a long time to study it out from the

Bible, and then they had to teach the brethren near them, and then they had to get the money to pay for the paper. So it was in the early part of 1846 that they published this light on the sanctuary in *The Day Dawn*.

They sent it out to all the believers whose names they could find. And very soon back came letters, some of them thanking God for the light, others doubting. Among them was a letter from James White, and another from Joseph Bates. Each of these men, one in Maine, the other in Massachusetts, had received a copy of the paper.

"You have the truth," each of them wrote; "we endorse what you have written about the sanctuary. Can we not have a conference of those who believe this new light, that we may be firmly united?"

So the brethren in western New York [175] appointed a conference to be held at Hiram Edson's place, and invited James White and Joseph Bates to come. Both tried to come, but White could not, and only Bates came from the East.

Joseph Bates had another message.

They had a good time studying the sanctuary question, and found joy together in this light God had given. But Joseph Bates had another message. He talked to them about their duty to keep the seventh day as the Sabbath. For you [176] know they had all been keeping Sunday before this. And one day he preached to them on the Sabbath question, showing them that God set apart the seventh day at creation for His holy Sabbath, and that it had never been taken away, only people had begun to keep Sunday, a heathen holiday, in its place.

When Joseph Bates had finished, Edson arose and said, "I thank God I have found a man who can stand up and say, 'seventh-day Sabbath.' I stand with you side by side."

Then Crosier arose and said, "Better go slowly, brethren, better go slowly. Let us be cautious, and not step upon new planks until we know whether they will hold us up or not."

"I have been studying the question of the Sabbath for a long time," answered Edson, "and for my part I have put my weight on it, and I know it is a plank that will hold us up."

And Doctor Hahn said, "That's the truth," and his wife said, "It is the truth," and several others also at that time stood up for the Sabbath. But Crosier, though for a time he kept the Sabbath, soon gave it up, and after this he walked no more with the brethren.

Now why do you suppose Joseph Bates was preaching about the Sabbath, and who was supporting him? Well, that's the next story. [177]

"Joseph, I haven't enough flour to finish the baking."

XV

THE SABBATH

There is a bridge across the Acushnet River, in Massachusetts, connecting Fairhaven with New Bedford. Now it is a steel and concrete bridge; a hundred years ago it was a wooden bridge. And it was nearly a hundred years ago that, on a spring morning, two old friends met on that wooden bridge.

"What's the news, Captain Bates?" sang out Mr. Hall.

And Captain Bates replied, "The news is that the seventh day is the Sabbath."

This was not the news that Mr. Hall was expecting. He had thought that perhaps he would hear that the "Eliza Jane" was in port, or that the good brig "Empress" had brought in a cargo worth thirty thousand dollars, or perhaps that Captain Bates had felt a twinge of rheumatism (which would be news indeed!) or that Texas had come into the Union. But Captain Bates's mind was filled with more important things. He had but now come back from a visit to the little company of Adventists in Washington, New Hampshire, who he had heard were [179] keeping the seventh-day Sabbath. They had been taught by Rachel Preston, a Seventh Day Baptist, and a number of them had started keeping the Sabbath. Captain Bates was convinced by the Bible evidence they showed him. Strange, he thought, that a thing so clear in the law of God should have been hidden to his eyes so long. But now that he saw, he must declare.

"The news, Brother Hall," he said, "is that the seventh day is the Sabbath of the Lord our God."

"Well," said Mr. Hall, "I'll go home and study my Bible on that." He did; and the next time be met Captain Bates, he reported that both he and his wife were also keeping the Sabbath.

Pioneer Stories

This was in the spring of 1845, and so you see that Joseph Bates had been keeping the Sabbath for over a year when he went to the conference at the home of Hiram Edson and testified there concerning it. Shortly after that conference he decided that he must write a book or pamphlet about the true Sabbath; for he knew that he could send this truth much better if he had it printed, since books could go to a thousand places while he was going to one.

Yet how could he write a book? He was as poor as Himes when the *Signs of the Times* was [180] started. Perhaps he was poorer; he had only a York shilling,—twelve and a half cents. When he accepted the second advent message he was worth about eleven thousand dollars; but, believing with all his heart that Jesus was soon coming, he sold off his property and used the money in giving the message. And now he had nothing left but this York shilling.

However, he prayed about the matter, and he felt assured that God wanted him to write the little book about the Sabbath. So he sat down at his desk, with his Bible before him, and began to write, He had not gone very far in his writing when his wife, coming in from the kitchen, opened the door and said, "Joseph, I haven't enough flour to finish the baking."

"How much flour do you lack?" asked her husband.

"About four pounds," she said.

"Very well," said he. And getting up, he took a six-quart milk pan from the kitchen shelf, went out to the grocery store, and bought a panful of flour. He took it home, put it in the kitchen while his wife was out, and went back to his writing.

In no time Mrs. Bates came in again. "Joseph," said she, "where did this flour come from?" [181]

"Why," said he, "isn't there enough? You *said* you wanted four pounds."

"Yes," said she, "but where did you get it?"

"I bought it," said he.

"You, Captain Bates, a man who has sailed vessels out of New Bedford to all parts of the world, have been out and *bought four pounds* of flour!"

"Wife," said Joseph Bates, "I spent for that flour the last money I have on earth."

Mrs. Bates threw her apron up to her eyes, and began to cry. She had not known before that her husband had spent the last of his money in the cause.

The Sabbath

Sobbing bitterly, she cried, "What are we going to do?"

Joseph Bates arose, and standing up to his full height, be said impressively, "I am going to write a book, and I am going to circulate it, and spread this Sabbath truth before the world."

"Well, but," said Mrs. Bates, still weeping, "what are we going to live on?"

"The Lord is going to open the way," answered her husband smilingly.

"Yes, 'the Lord is going to open the way,'" she returned. "That's what you always say." And bursting into a fresh flood of tears, she left the room.

Joseph Bates sat down and began writing [182] again on his Sabbath pamphlet. In about half an hour it was impressed on his mind that there was a letter at the post office for him, and he should go and get it. So he went out, and down to the post office.

"Is there a letter for me, Mr. Drew?" he asked.

The postmaster looked. "Yes, there is, Captain Bates," he said; "postage due, five cents." In those days people could pay the postage when they sent the letter, or not, just as they pleased. If they didn't, it had to be paid by the person to whom the letter was sent. And here was the postage to be paid, and Bates hadn't a cent.

"Mr. Drew," he said to the postmaster, "I am out of money; I haven't even the five cents to pay the postage. But will you let me see where the letter is from?"

"Oh, that's all right, Captain Bates," said the postmaster, "take it along and pay some other time," and he handed him the letter.

"No," said Bates, "I will not take the letter from the post office until the postage is paid." It was a principle of his not to go into debt.

But he looked at the letter, and said, "I feel that there is money in this letter." And handing it back to the postmaster, he asked, "Will you [183] please open it? If there is money in it, you take the postage out; if not, I will not read it."

The postmaster opened it, and the first thing to meet his eye was a ten-dollar bill! He made change, took out the postage, and gave the rest of the money, with the letter, over to Joseph Bates. It was from a man who said in the letter that the Lord had impressed his mind that Captain Bates needed money.

Joseph Bates walked off down town, bought a barrel of flour and some potatoes and sugar and other things, called a drayman, and told him to take the things up to his house. "Probably my wife will tell you the goods don't belong there, but don't you pay any attention to what she says. Unload the goods just as I have told you, on the front porch."

"Yes, Captain," said the drayman, "I will do just as you have ordered."

Then Bates went down to the printing office and hired them to print one thousand pamphlets for him as quickly as they could. This was to be the Sabbath book. He said he would pay as fast as he had the money, and would take no books from the office until all were paid for. Where he would get the money, he didn't know, but he was sure the Lord would send it to him.

He stopped on his way home to buy some [184] paper and pens, and by the time he reached his house the groceries had come and were on the front porch. He went in at the back door, and sat down at his desk again. Pretty soon in came his wife in great excitement, and said, "Joseph, just look out there. Where did that stuff come from? A drayman drove up here and just would unload it. I told him it didn't belong here, that we had no money with which to buy such things, but he declared this was the exact number where it was to be left. And he left it all, and drove off."

"Well," said her husband, "I guess it's all right."

"But where did it come from?" she persisted.

"Why," said he, "the Lord sent it."

"Oh, yes," she answered, "'the Lord sent it'; that's what you always say."

Then he handed the letter to her, and said, "Read this, and you will learn where it came from." She read it, and then she went out for another cry, but that was because she was ashamed of her lack of faith. And pretty soon she came back and asked her husband's forgiveness.

Joseph Bates wrote his book, the printer printed it, and the money came in for it, all in good time. H. S. Gurney, who you remember went with Joseph Bates on his trip in the South, [185] received some money on a debt he had thought would never be paid, and with a part of this he paid the last of the printing bill. And with the book the truth began to spread more and more.

So Joseph Bates began to teach among the Adventists the truth of the Sabbath. And as you shall see in the stories that follow, the Lord blessed his self-sacrifice, and soon brought greater light and power from heaven for the teaching of this testing truth. And those who from this time on came together in the faith of the Lord's coming, the heavenly sanctuary service, and the seventh-day Sabbath, made the first of the people who have come to be known by the name Seventh-day Adventists. [186]

XVI

THE SPIRIT OF PROPHECY

Before the passing of the time, God gave first to one young man, then to another, a vision which would have prepared His people to understand their disappointment and the work remaining for them to do. But these young men, each in turn, refused to give the message because they did not understand it. Later, at different times, each of them heard the same message given by the third one whom God chose, and it was recalled to their minds that this was the message that was given to them but which they had neglected. Who this third messenger was I will tell you.

Not two months had gone by after the passing of the time, when one day at morning worship five women were kneeling in prayer. One of these was Ellen Harmon. You remember how frail and sick this young girl had been ever since her accident. But she had believed Jesus was coming on the tenth day of the seventh month, and this hope had kept her up. Since the passing of the time she had grown worse very fast. The doctor said she had consumption, that one lung was [187] useless and the other almost so. He said she would die in a very short time. At night she could lie down, but had to be bolstered up with pillows, in order to sleep at all. Often she would be awakened with coughing, and bleeding from the lungs. Her voice was almost gone.

This morning, as these five were bowed together, Ellen began in a whisper to pray. She did not yet understand why Jesus had not come, and with these sisters she was praying earnestly for light about it. As she prayed, God came down by His Holy Spirit. All felt the influence, but Ellen most of all. In a mo-

The Spirit of Prophecy

ment she passed out of knowledge of things around her. She felt the power of God more than she had before in her dreams. Light and glory seemed all about her, and as though on wings she felt herself rising higher and higher from the earth.

She looked for fellow believers, to see If they were going too, but she could not find them. Then a voice said, "Look again, and look a little higher." She raised her eyes, and saw a long, narrow path, high above the earth. It led on to the Holy City, far up the path. Behind them was a light set, and an angel told her that was "The Midnight Cry." Some of the people on the path denied that the light behind them, which was shining now on their way, was true, and [188] shortly they stumbled and fell off the path to the dark world below.

Soon the faithful ones heard the voice of God telling them the day and hour when Jesus would come. All the people traveling on the path now numbered just one hundred forty-four thousand. At this time she saw them surrounded by wicked men, who would rush up to catch them and put them into prison, or to kill them; but when they tried to do it, they would fall helpless.

Very soon the waiting ones saw in the east a small black cloud, about half as large as a man's hand. It was the cloud of angels coming with Jesus. As it drew nearer, it grew lighter and lighter, until it was a great white cloud. Fire glowed below it, and a rainbow stretched over it. Then they could see Jesus in plain view, sitting on the cloud. "His hair was white and curly, and lay on His shoulders; and upon His head were many crowns. His feet had the appearance of fire; in His right hand was a sharp sickle, in His left a silver trumpet." His bright eyes seemed to pierce through every soul; but, though the faces of the righteous paled, there was no sin in them, and Jesus' gaze upon them was loving, and He said, "Those who have clean hands and pure hearts shall be able to stand; My [190] grace is sufficient for you." All their faces lighted up, and they shouted and sang.

Then Jesus, wrapped in flames of glory, came near to the earth on the cloud. He put His silver trumpet to His lips, and far, far over all the earth it sounded. And He cried, "Awake, awake, awake! ye that sleep in the dust, and arise." The earth heaved in a great earthquake, the graves opened, and from land and sea the righteous dead came forth to meet their living friends and the angels and Jesus.

She raised her eyes, and saw a long narrow path, high above the earth,

The Spirit of Prophecy

When Ellen had seen these things in vision, an angel seemed to bear her gently down again to this dark world. When she came out of vision, she found herself in the midst of her four friends, still at the worship hour.

Very soon after this, another vision was given her, in which the angel told her she must go and tell the people what the Lord revealed to her. She was shown that many people would hate her, that she would have to endure sickness and evil words and hatred, but that God would sustain her.

This vision greatly troubled her, for it told her that she, a seventeen-year-old girl, small, frail, and timid, must go out into the world and teach people, very often that which they did not wish to hear. It seemed she could not do it. [191] She was sick, and so hoarse she could talk only in a whisper.

So she prayed for several days, far into the night, that the Lord would not require her to do this. But all the answer she received, just as had William Miller, was, "Make known to others what I have revealed to you." She longed

The church gathered to pray for her.

to die. Naturally she wanted to be loved, not hated; sick, she wanted to shrink out of sight, not push forward in talking to people and teaching them.

At last the church in Portland, to whom she had told her first vision, all gathered to pray for her, and they encouraged her. She was taken off in vision again, and a bright angel said to her these words from Jesus: "Make known to others what I have revealed to you."

"But," she cried, "I am afraid. I have seen others who have told what the Lord had revealed to them, and they became so proud over it that they sinned, and God left them. I am afraid I shall do the same. Oh, if I must go," she cried, "will not the Lord keep me from becoming proud and sinful?"

"Your prayer is heard," said the angel; "if you are in danger of becoming proud and self exalted, God will save you. He will stretch out His hand upon you and smite you down in sickness, and so draw you to Himself and keep you [192] humble. Deliver the message faithfully. Endure to the end, and you shall eat the fruit of the tree of life, and drink of the water of life."

So Ellen was encouraged, and from this time on she was faithful in giving her unpopular message. [193]

In the black field above is shown the "kite," containing the belt and sword of Orion, the arrow pointing to the "gap." The larger map is a greatly enlarged illustration of the "gap."

XVII

THE OPENING HEAVENS AND THE UNCHANGED LAW

Joseph Bates had come up for a conference at Topsham, Maine. It was in November, 1846, over two years after the disappointment. Some of the others present were James White, J. N. Andrews, H. S. Gurney (with whom Bates had worked in the South), and Ellen Harmon. Three months before, she and James White had been married. Thus she was given by the Lord a strong protector, on whom in her weakness she might lean, but to whom also she was to be the greatest strength. You know from what I have told you how strong and fearless and devoted James White had been, and you know how faithful Miss Harmon had been in the work God had given her to do. But perhaps you do not know, as they could not know then, how great and mighty was to be the work they should accomplish in the years to come. From this time on we know Ellen Harmon as Mrs. Ellen G. White.

At this time Mrs. White did not see the importance of keeping the seventh-day Sabbath, which Joseph Bates urged, and Joseph Bates was [195] not sure that the visions of Mrs. White were from the Lord, though he was sure she was a good and faithful Christian who believed what she told. And here the Lord brought them both, and all the brethren with them, to believe the truth each had.

Bates had been, as you remember, a captain of ships on the sea. All seamen study the stars, for these are often about all they have to see, and the captains have to sail their vessels, oftentimes, by the positions of the stars. So Captain

The Opening Heavens and the Unchanged Law

[196] Bates was a great lover of astronomy, which means the study of the stars and other bodies in the sky. Mrs. White, on the other hand, knew nothing about it, for you remember how she was kept from school. And when Joseph Bates tried to talk with her about the heavenly bodies, she could not understand very much, and told him she had never looked into a book on astronomy.

They had come up for a conference at Topsham, Maine.

But one day, here in the conference, she was taken off in vision when he was present, and for the first time the Lord showed her some of the planets, which are worlds much like our own. Through telescopes men have discovered many things about them which we cannot see with our naked eyes. For instance, Jupiter, the largest of the planets near us, has not one moon, as we have, but four; while Saturn, another planet, has at least eight, though only seven had been discovered then. And up in its sky it has great beautiful bands of different colors which extend all the way around it.

In vision, then, Mrs. White was taken to see these planets, and as she talked about them, describing them, Captain Bates, his face wreathed in smiles, would say, "Now she is viewing Jupiter," and, "She is describing Saturn," and so on. She told much more than astronomers knew about these, for they are not sure the [197] planets are inhabited, but she saw that they are. On Saturn she saw good old Enoch, who was translated five thousand years ago, without dying. He said that was not his home, that he was only visiting there, that he lived in heaven, where God dwells, and there he was waiting until the earth should be restored as it had been in Eden. The people of these worlds were all very much more beautiful and strong than the people of earth, for sin has never entered there.

But after seeing the planets, she seemed to pass over a great distance in the heavens, until she came to the place that is called "the gap in the sky." When she began to describe this, Elder Bates rose to his feet in great excitement. "She is giving a more wonderful description," be said, "than any astronomer ever dreamed of." And still she spoke of its great beauty, with the four great stars far apart as its gates, and the glory, the wonderful glory, shining through. The heavens beyond, she said, made a region more enlightened. This indeed is the gateway from our part of the universe into the central heaven where God dwells.

I am sure you want to know where this wonderful gap in the sky is. It will not look to you at all like a gap when you see it. You would have to look through the most powerful telescope [198] in all the world to see much, and then you could not see as much as she saw in vision. To us it looks just like a faint star, but through the scope it shown to be a very glorious place, with many great stars in it, and a place of wonderful light in the center. Now let me tell you how to find it in the sky, though you can probably never see anything of its glory until in the company of Jesus you pass through it on the way to heaven.

In the wintertime,—for in midsummer you cannot see it at all,—in the wintertime, if you look up into the sky toward the south, about half way up to the zenith (the top of the sky) you will find a group of six stars, shaped somewhat like a kite with a tail. At least that is what I thought of when I was a boy. At the end of the last chapter you will find a picture of the group, and another of the gap in the sky as it looks through a telescope. Astronomers call the four stars that make the square, "the belt of Orion," and the lowest of the four,

The Opening Heavens and the Unchanged Law

with the two below it, they call "the sword of Orion." The middle one of these three stars is fainter than the other two, as you will see. It looks rather hazy. It is not really one star, but a great many, millions upon millions of miles apart, only they are so far away from us that they look like one star. And in the [199] middle of them all there are four stars, which are still millions upon millions of miles apart. And all in between these four there is a glorious light, the light of the great heaven beyond. This is

"the gap in the sky."

So always in the winter evenings, more than all the stars I watch this star in the sword of Orion, remembering that through this "gap in the sky" Jesus will come. That makes it seem nearer, just as if the way home were being pointed out to me. In November you will see this group of stars rising in the southeast about nine o'clock. It rises earlier and earlier as the days go on, until in May you will probably lose sight of it altogether, it sets so soon after the sun has set.

Well, when Joseph Bates heard this vision, he was very happy. He was sure now that the Lord must be giving the visions, for he had been made sure before that Mrs. White knew nothing of astronomy, and here she was telling more than he knew. And he said he was the happiest man alive.

A few weeks after this, while still at Topsham, Mrs. White was given another vision, in which she saw the sanctuary in heaven in the same form as it had been on earth. In the first room of the sanctuary she saw the altar of [200] incense, the candlestick with seven lamps, and the table of showbread. Then Jesus raised the veil that separated it from the Most Holy Place, and she entered. There she saw an ark of purest gold, over which stood two shining cherubs or angels, their faces turned toward each other, and looking down in reverence upon the ark. Over the ark was a brightness that appeared like the throne of God. Jesus stood there, and as the prayers of His people on earth came up to Him, He offered them up before God, with the incense from His censer.

Then she saw the ark opened, and within it was the law of God, the Ten Commandments written on tables of stone. To her astonishment, as she looked upon these ten great words, she saw the fourth commandment encircled with greater, more brilliant, light than the others, for it is the great commandment which holds men to God. If everybody had always truly kept the Sabbath,

Pioneer Stories

there would never have been a heathen in the world, nor an infidel; for the Sabbath reminds us of the God who is the Creator and Redeemer. God has never changed His command which says, "The seventh day is the Sabbath of the Lord thy God; in it thou shalt not do any work."But Satan has brought men to leave the Sabbath and to take a heathen holiday in its [201] place. Thus, without knowing it, many dishonor God.

The ark opened, and within it the law of God.

After she had had this vision, the matter seemed very different to Mrs. White. She had been keeping Sunday, and thought it didn't matter much which day was kept. But now she and James White, her husband, began at once to keep the Sabbath and to study this truth in the Bible. And so they were united with Joseph Bates, and he with them. Thus at last these three servants of God were brought fully together for their great work. [203]

Annie took a seat by the door.

XVIII

TWO NEW WORKERS

Mrs. Rebecca Smith of West Wilton, New Hampshire, had just received the truth of the Sabbath from Joseph Bates. She had two children, a young man and a young woman, who were both in school away from home, and she was very anxious about them. They had all believed in the coming of Jesus in 1844, but since the disappointment, Uriah and Annie had seemed to be drifting into the world. The mother had been praying for them, and now that she knew the truth of the Sabbath, she was more anxious than ever that they be saved for this work.

"I am going to hold a meeting at Somerville, Massachusetts, in a few days," said Mr. Bates. Now Annie was in school at Charleston, Mass., two miles from Somerville. "You write to Annie," said Mr. Bates, "and ask her to attend that meeting at the house of Paul Folsom, and I will see her. By the Lord's blessing she may receive the truth. Let us both pray, in the meantime, that God will move upon her heart to go."

Annie read her mother's letter. "It's going [205] to be on Saturday," she said to herself, "and there's no school that day. Well, just to please mother, I'll go."

The night before that Sabbath she dreamed a dream. She thought she went to the meeting, but was late, and that when she reached there they were singing the second hymn. Every seat was filled except one next to the door, and she sat down in that. A tall, noble-looking, pleasant man was pointing to a queer-looking chart, and saying, "Unto two thousand three hundred days; then shall the sanctuary be cleansed." What he said was very interesting, she dreamed, and she knew it was the truth.

The same night Joseph Bates had a dream. He dreamed he was in the room

Two New Workers

where the meeting was to be held. He dreamed that he changed his mind about the subject he was to give, and that be spoke on the sanctuary question. After they had sung the first hymn and prayed, and were singing the second hymn, the door opened, and a young lady came in and took the only vacant seat, by the door. It was Annie R. Smith, he dreamed, and she became interested at once and accepted the faith.

So they both awoke that Sabbath morning, and they both forgot all about their dreams. Annie made ready to go to the meeting in plenty [206] of time, but in Somerville she missed her way, and by the time she found Mr. Folsom's house, it was late. As she went in, they were singing the second hymn, and she took the only seat left, right by the door. Joseph Bates stood up and pointed to the chart, quoting, "Unto two thousand and three hundred days; then shall the sanctuary be cleansed." Instantly Annie's dream flashed into her mind. At the same time Mr. Bates saw her, and his dream came back to him. He sent up a prayer for special help. He explained to the people how the disappointment came about, because the sanctuary is in heaven, not on this earth, and then he showed how the third message must be given, and brought forward the truth of the Sabbath.

After the meeting closed, he stepped up to Annie and said, with a welcoming smile, "I believe this is Sister Smith's daughter, of West Wilton. I never saw you before, but your face looks familiar. I dreamed of seeing you last night."

"Why," said Annie, "I dreamed of seeing you. I dreamed of being in this meeting, and everything has happened just as I dreamed it. And," she added, with a little hesitation, "I dreamed it was the truth; and now I know it is the truth." [207]

They had a good, glad visit, and when Annie went away, she had made up her mind to keep the Sabbath and give up her other plans. She and her brother had been offered a place to teach at one thousand dollars a year and their board, but now she gave that up. Going back to her school in Charleston, she packed her trunk and went home to her mother, not to stay there in idleness, but, as you will see to enter very soon a great work.

Her brother Uriah did not receive the message then. But the next year, in

September, there was a conference near his home, and impressed by Annie's conversion, he went to attend it. On his return home, he carefully studied what he had heard, and in December he began to keep the Sabbath.

His sister Annie had gone over a year before to help James White in the publishing of his paper, and the next spring Uriah also went to Rochester, New York, where the *Advent Review and Sabbath Herald* was being published, and began to work for it.

They did not receive much, only their board and clothing, which cost little. And this they did gladly for the sake of the truth, instead of getting one thousand dollars and their board, as they might have by teaching in the school. [208]

For fifty years he was an editor.

Uriah Smith soon began to write, and for fifty years he was editor of the *Review and Herald*, still being hard at work for the paper and the cause at the time he died, in 1903. God has greatly blessed his early sacrifice and his devotion, and many, many thousands have been converted by the work he has done. He has written some of our most important books. Probably the one you know best is the work, "Thoughts on Daniel and the Revelation," which explains the prophecies of these wonderful books of the Bible. [209]

Two New Workers

Annie Smith did not live so long as her brother. She died in 1855, scarcely three years after she had come to work in the office. But while she lived, she was a great blessing and help, and her work has lived after her. Some of our most beautiful hymns were written by her. I hope you will watch for her name, and come to know many of her hymns. One song she wrote, No. 371 in the "Church Hymnal," tells the story of three of the pioneers in our work. The first stanza relates to Joseph Bates:

> "I saw one weary, sad, and torn,
> With eager steps press on the way."

The second stanza is about James White:

> "And one I saw, with sword and shield,
> Who boldly braved the world's cold frown."

And the third one is of John N. Andrews:

> "And there was one who left behind
> The cherished friends of early years,
> And honor, pleasure, wealth resigned,
> To tread the path bedewed with tears.
> Through trials deep and conflicts sore,
> Yet still a smile of joy he wore:
> I asked what buoyed his spirits up,
> 'O this!' said he, 'the blessed hope.'" [210]

XIX

PRINTING THE TRUTH

It was a plain room, unadorned with pictures, and without a carpet. A number of old chairs, no two alike, were all that could be called furniture. Two flour barrels stood a little distance apart, and upon them was laid a board. This was the table used for the daily meals, and for folding and mailing papers. Such was the appearance in the first days of the publishing work in Rochester, N. Y. As you know, Joseph Bates had before this gotten out a pamphlet about the Sabbath, and James White had from 1849 to 1851 published a paper in Middletown, Conn., Oswego, N. Y., Paris, Maine, and Saratoga Springs, N. Y. It was called *Present Truth* at first, but in Maine the name was changed to *The Second Advent Review and Sabbath Herald*, and in Saratoga Springs the word "Second" was dropped. So when they moved to Rochester, in 1852, the name of the paper was what it has ever since remained, *The Advent Review and Sabbath Herald*, or, for short, *The Review and Herald*.

In Rochester an old house had been rented by Mr. White for $175 a year, and this was one of [211] the rooms. In this house he and his family and their helpers lived, while they struggled to prepare the truth in tracts and pamphlets and in the new paper, *The Advent Review and Sabbath Herald*. They were too poor to buy good furniture. They had bought old bedsteads for twenty-five cents apiece, and ten old chairs, four of which had no seats.

The family could not afford high-priced food. Butter was too dear to be bought, and so were potatoes. They ate turnips in their place.

But the printing press and the type and the paper stock, these belonged to

Printing the Truth

the cause. For two years before, Mr. White had published the paper, first in Paris, Maine, and then in Saratoga, N. Y., but he had to hire the work done. Now Hiram Edson sold his farm and loaned the money to buy the needed things for the publishing work. It was only a little printing press, run by hand, there were only a few fonts of type, and the stock of paper was not great. But they were able to publish the paper twice a month, and they made tracts and pamphlets and small books.

Nowadays when books are printed, they come from great presses that print sixty-four pages at a time; the sheets are folded by machinery, then the folded sheets, called signatures, are gathered together, and another machine sews [212]

The printing press and the type belonged to the cause.

them, and still another trims the edges off smooth. But at first they had none of these machines in that office. To get out the first pamphlet, they made a "bee" of sisters Rochester, who with the few office hands folded the sheets, then gathered the signatures together, and John Loughborough stabbed holes in them with a pegging awl for the needle to pass through. Then, after they had been sewed by hand, Uriah Smith trimmed the edges with a straight edge and a sharp penknife. Later they bought some machines to do the work. [213]

And when the papers and the little books were to be sent out, they all gathered around the table and prayed with tears that God would bless them so that they might take the truth. And God did, so that hundreds began to keep the Sabbath, in New England and New York and Michigan and other western states. Brother Bates had made a trip into Michigan to preach, and he began to work at the city of Jackson.

The people who worked in the office, most of them, received only their board and a little more, just enough to clothe them. Only in this way could the work be kept up when they were so poor, for at that time they did not charge a price for the paper, but sent it out free, and only asked those who could to send in money.

Mr. White, Mrs. White, and Father Bates did most of the writing for the paper, though one by one others began to come in to help. There were Uriah Smith and J. N. Andrews, and J. N. Loughborough and J. H. Waggoner, and others more and more.

But upon James White fell the heaviest part of the work of writing for the paper. One time he and Mrs. White started together from Rochester to go to Maine, having meetings all along the way. They went with a horse and a buggy. Little Edson was very sick just before [214] they left. The cholera was killing hundreds of people. All night long, for weeks, they had heard the rumble of the hearses and carriages that were taking the dead to Mount Hope Cemetery. And now little Edson was attacked. But they prayed for him, and the Lord raised him up. Still he was very weak, but they would not stay for that, since the Lord had bidden them go. Putting their little boy on a pillow, they carried him with them, driving twenty miles the first day. The little fellow could not sleep, and his mother sat up rocking him all the night, though they must make a hard journey the next day. Satan was trying to turn them back by making their little boy sick, but they believed God had heard their prayers and they would not return.

The next day Mrs. White, being so worn out that she was afraid she would drop the child, put him in her lap and tied him to her waist, and they both slept most of the way, while Mr. White drove. Thus day after day they traveled. They would stop at places along the way, letting the horse eat by the roadside while they ate their own lunch. Then Mr. White would take out paper and pencil, and on the top of his hat or the top of the lunch-box be would write his articles for *The Review and Herald*, and send them back to Rochester to Uriah Smith, who would make [215] up the paper. Thus, while traveling and working very hard, did the pioneers in the cause keep up the work of publishing, that the message might go much farther and faster than they could carry it themselves. [216]

They both slept most of the way.

XX

MOVING TO MICHIGAN

Joseph Bates in 1849 made a visit to Michigan. There were no Sabbath-keepers in Michigan then. Stopping at Jackson, in the south-central part of the state, he visited among the people, and soon interested quite a good many in the truths he taught. This company at Jackson made the first church in the West. They were very happy in their new faith, and worked hard to give a knowledge of it to others, so only a few years had passed before the cause in Michigan began to grow strong. And these brethren helped in paying expenses at the office, and in supporting men to go out preaching the message at that time when there was the greatest need.

In 1853 Mr. and Mrs. White made a visit to Michigan, and held meetings in many places. The country was new then, and had a great many swamps in it. The roads had often to go through these swamps, and to make the road firm

The roads had often to go through swamps.

Moving to Michigan

the road builders used to lay logs crosswise on it close together. Over these they would pile earth and muck from the swamp. This was called a corduroy road. But in wet weather [217] much of this earth would be carried away or be washed down between the logs, so that it would leave great bumps and hollows. And sometimes a poor log would rot out, and leave a bigger hole than ever. The people called these holes "thank-you-ma'ams." That was a cheerful way of meeting them; for when, riding over the broken corduroy road in a wagon, they would go bump, bump, bumpity-bump, and away down k-plunk, until their bones cracked and their teeth snapped, then instead of scolding and complaining, they would screw their faces into wry smiles, and murmur pleasantly, "Thank you, ma'am," as though the road had done them a favor.

Over such roads Mr. and Mrs. White went through many parts of the state. There was just one railroad through the state at this time, and [218] that the people called "the huckleberry road," because they said the conductor would stop the train whenever it went through a huckleberry swamp, and let the passengers off to eat berries. That was only their way of telling how slow and irregular the trains were.

They built a small two-story printing house in Battle Creek.

But however poor the country was, the people had good hearts, and the truth found many friends who would hold it up. Most of the traveling through the state had to be done by wagon; and over the roads, many parts of them corduroy, Mr. and Mrs. White drove in their weakness (for Mr. White at this

"Buck and Bill are pullin' away."

Moving to Michigan

time was not strong), and they held many meetings, so the cause grew greatly.

In 1855 the friends in Michigan agreed together to ask Brother White to move the [219] publishing work to Michigan. Four men, Dan Palmer, Cyrenius Smith, J. P. Kellogg, and Henry Lyons, made up $1200, bought a lot in the little city of Battle Creek, fifty miles west of Jackson, and built a small two-story house, twenty feet wide and thirty feet long. This was the beginning of the work in Battle Creek, which afterwards grew so large.

Here, then, in the fall, Mr. White moved the printing office, and from this time on the work grew rapidly. They soon bought a large press, to be run by steam, and other machinery. The books and papers and tracts began to multiply and spread the truth.

The few Seventh-day Adventists then living there sacrificed a great deal in order to help the cause. There was one man, a farmer who made up his mind to help when a printing press was called for. But he had no money to spare, so he sold his yoke of oxen, Buck and Bill, and gave the money to the publishing house for the buying of the press. It made him happy to do it; for in this way, be said, his oxen were helping pull the chariot of truth along. And every time he passed the Review and Herald office and heard the press running, he would stop to chuckle, and say, "Buck and Bill are pullin' away, they're *pu-u ullin' away*!" [220]

And all the work was done by sacrifice. Many who wrote did it for no pay at all, some of them working with their hands part of the time at farming or carpentry or something else to pay their expenses.

One of the ministers tells how he worked with his tent in Illinois for three winter months. He got his board, a ten-dollar buffalo overcoat, and ten dollars in money. Then be walked part way home, a good many miles, in order to have a little of the money left. And he says, "My case was not an exception: other ministers fared equally well, and we were all happy in the Lord's work."

From this time on for over fifty years, the headquarters of the work were in Battle Creek, Mich. Many people came into the faith in the western states,— Michigan, Ohio, Indiana, Illinois, Wisconsin, Iowa, and beyond; and so for many years the West more than the East saw the rapid development of the work. [222]

XXI

PREACHING IN POVERTY

One of the early converts who became a power in the work, was John N. Loughborough. He had been in the '44 movement, and when scarcely seventeen, he preached the doctrine.

At that time, he was sick with fever and ague, but he felt impressed that he must preach. And as soon as he had made up his mind to do it, the chills left him. He had no money left, however, and very little clothing. How could he go out to preach? Well, a neighbor offered to let him saw wood, as much as he could in his weakness; and doing this, he saved one dollar. The same neighbor, a big six-footer, was so kind as to give him a vest and a pair of trousers. But John Loughborough had a small body, and he found the trousers seven inches too long! Seven inches were cut off, but still the trousers made no very nice fit. On they went, however, and the big vest as well. His brother gave him a double-breasted overcoat which had been cut short, and this did for a coat. Thus fitted out, young John Loughborough started out to preach, going thirty miles away from home to start in. [223]

The first house he stopped at was that of a family interested in the prophecies. They welcomed him, and bade him take off his overcoat. Blushing and stammering, he had to explain that it was not his overcoat, but his coat. If his friends thought he looked rather odd, what would the scoffers say when, in the pulpit, he stood up to preach, wearing his double-breasted short overcoat and his big baggy trousers?

However, he would not back out, and on the evening after New Year be

Preaching in Poverty

opened meetings in the Baptist church. The people crowded in to hear him, and he was able to tell the truth with power. The second evening he preached to a still larger congregation. The next day he was invited to visit a family, and when he reached there, he found a good many people present. Very soon a minister came in, and looking the young preacher over condescendingly, he said:

"You had a large attendance last night?"

"Yes," said Mr. Loughborough, "and they seemed much interested."

"I don't know," returned the minister, "I guess they had a curiosity to hear a boy preach. Did I understand you to say that the soul is not immortal?"

"I said so," answered the boy.

This was a new truth to the Adventists, a [224] truth which George Storrs had brought out. Not all of the Adventists took it for truth, but John Loughborough had read Storrs' pamphlet, and he believed it.

"Well," said the minister, "what do you do with the text that says, 'These shall go away into everlasting punishment, the death that never dies'?"

"Sir," said the boy preacher, "one half of your text is in the hymnbook instead of the Bible. The expression, 'death that never dies,' is not in the Bible. In Matthew 25:46 we read of everlasting punishment, but that is made plain by reading 2 Thessalonians 1:9, where it is called everlasting destruction."

"Yes," said the minister, "I understand that, but there is a text that reads as I said, and it is in the twenty-fifth chapter of Revelation."

"My good sir," returned Mr. Loughborough, "there are only twenty-two chapters in Revelation. Your text must be three chapters outside the Bible!"

The minister drew up to his full height, and he looked very high indeed beside "the boy." "I tell you it is in the twenty-fifth chapter of Revelation," he thundered. "Let me take your Bible, and I'll show you."

He took the Bible, and began turning over [225] the leaves of the Old Testament. "Where is Revelation?" he said at last.

John Loughborough took the Bible and turned to the last, the twenty-second chapter of Revelation. The minister looked at it for a moment, and then said, "Yes, I see. I should like to talk with you, but I have an engagement," and he hastily left the room. He had told the people there that he would show the boy preacher in two minutes where he was wrong. But though he had read

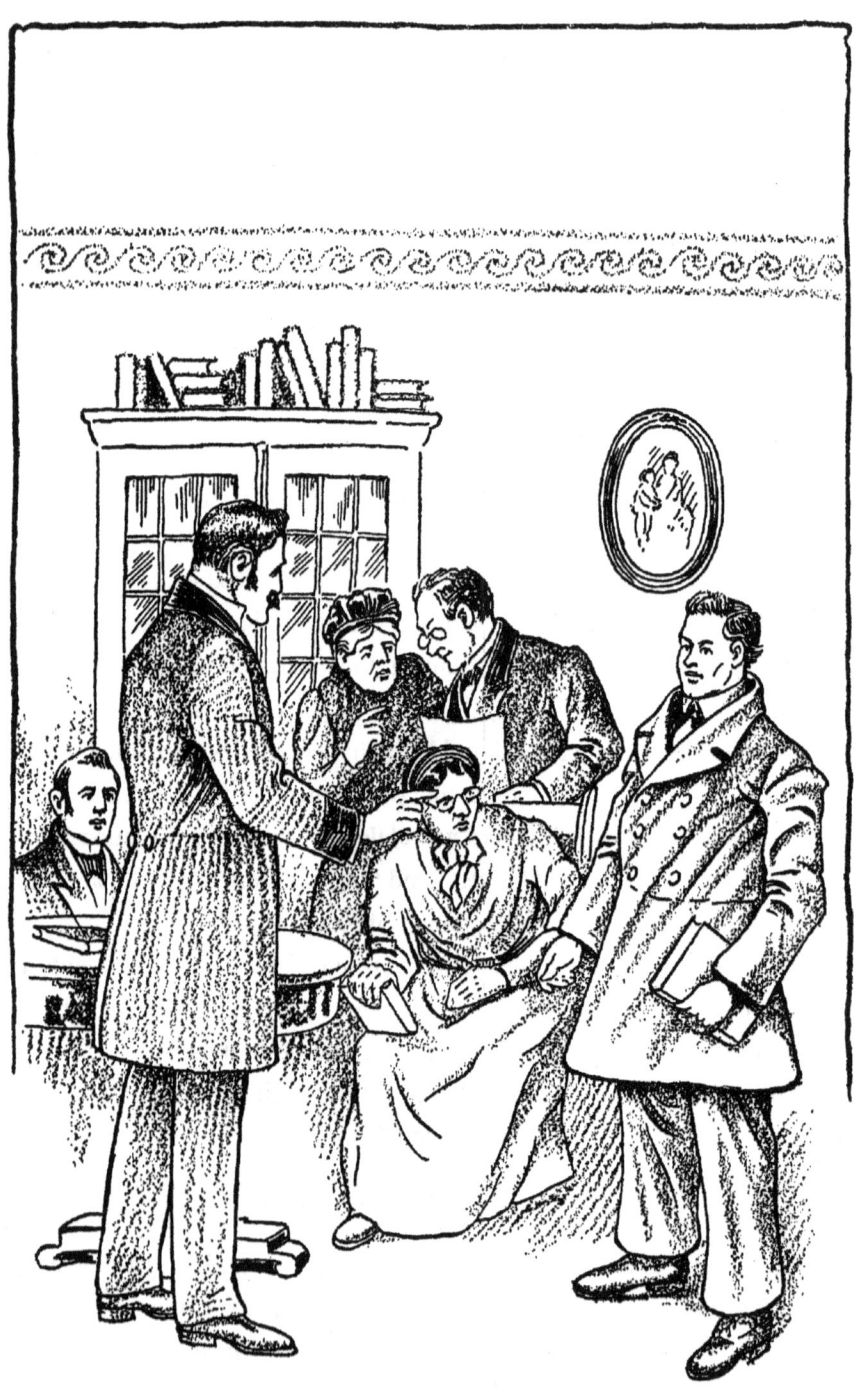

"Yes," said the minister, "but my text is in the twenty-fifth chapter of Revelation."

Preaching in Poverty

many books, he had not read his Bible enough.

When Mr. and Mrs. White came to Rochester, in 1852, John Loughborough heard the Sabbath message, and accepted it. Soon after, he began to preach that message, and through hardships about as great as those of his early experience, he helped to carry on the work.

At about the same time (1851), another man, away in the West, received the faith. His name was J. H. Waggoner. He too was one of those who did great service for Jesus in the advent message before be died. He wrote some powerful tracts and books that have helped many people into the light. But to show you how the ministers then often worked without much support, you want to see him one day in Michigan, as he comes into a believer's house, his boots worn out, [227] his coat threadbare, and his trousers frayed and worn. For he was preaching without pay, and his own money was now gone.

Another minister, named Hutchins, also happened to be at the home of this man, who was a farmer. Mr. Waggoner, tired out, had gone in to lie on the bed.

Said the farmer in a low voice to Mr. [228] Hutchins, "It's too bad for Brother Waggoner to go dressed like that."

"Well," answered Mr. Hutchins, "I have no doubt he would be better dressed if he had any money."

"Well, I'm sorry for him," sighed the brother.

"How sorry?" asked Mr. Hutchins. "Are you sorry enough to sell some of your wheat or oats to help him?"

"I don't know," said the man, shaking his bead. "Wheat is only sixty-five cents a bushel, and it ought never to be sold for that. Oats is only thirty-five cents. I don't want to sell any at that price; it would be too much of a sacrifice."

"Brother," said Mr. Hutchins, "don't you think that in those days when the Lord told the people to take a lamb of the first year and burn it up, they thought it was too bad, and that they would rather keep it a year or two, and get a fleece from it before making an offering of it?"

The brother shook his head again. "I do feel sorry for Elder Waggoner, but I don't see how I can sell any of my grain to help him."

"How much would you let him have if you had the money?"

"Oh, I'd let him have seven or eight dollars."

"I'll let you have the money to give him," said Mr. Hutchins, "as I happen to have a little [229] on hand; and when I need it, I'll ask you for it."

So the brother took the money and gave it to Mr. Waggoner, and of course it helped a little.

Do you suppose Mr. Waggoner did more than eight dollars' worth of good to that man? I'm afraid the man didn't get eight dollars' worth of good out of his gift; for it cost him no sacrifice. David said that he would not offer to God that which cost him nothing. The people were indebted to Mr. Waggoner, and such ministers as he, thousands of times more than they could ever pay. At the

"It's too bad for Brother Waggoner to go dressed like that."

same time, all the good such ministers did for the people, they did only to pay a debt; for they, as you and I, were debtors to Christ.

Listen: when Jesus gives us eternal, and the wonderful bliss of heaven and the new earth, He gives them as a gift, not as pay. He died in our place, and with all we can do we can never pay that debt. So people whom we may help don't owe us anything; but they owe Christ, for whom we are working, and when they give money or anything else, they must give it to Christ, who is our Master.

I am sure Mr. Waggoner realized this; and with the other ministers he endured his hardships cheerfully, saying "My Master, Jesus, had not where to lay His head." [230]

XXII

THE HEALTH WORK

Early in the history of Seventh-day Adventists God began to teach the people how to live healthfully, so that they might be able to do His work well. Mrs. White gave much instruction on the matter, and taught the right way of living and the natural means of healing. Joseph Bates was one of the first to practice what we know as "health reform." When he died, a hale, hearty old man of seventy-six, he had been keeping his health perfectly for many years on a diet of fruits, grains, nuts, and vegetables.

But diet, or what we eat, is not all there is to health reform. If we live right, God promises to keep us from disease, and if any are sick, He says His power is set in the church to heal them. But at the same time He wants us to know and to use all natural ways of making sick people well.

Let me tell you how this part of the truth came to one family, and that will show you how it came to many.

There was mourning in the home of Horace Lawrence, the elder of the church at Bangor, [231] N. Y. Mrs. Lawrence was very, very sick, and the brethren and sisters from all the neighboring towns in Franklin County who came to see her (for she had visited them many times, and some of them had learned the message through her work) were told she was too sick to see them.

"Oh, I'm so sorry," exclaimed one rosy-cheeked farmer's wife, standing in the Lawrence kitchen with her hand on a basket of fresh eggs she had brought. "I've driven away over from [232] Brandon to see her. I do hope the Lord will have mercy on dear Sister Lawrence. Can she eat anything?"

"No," answered Mr. Lawrence, "the doctor has us give her a little glass of wine every two hours, and that is all she can take to keep her alive."

"Can't you pray for her?" asked the sister.

Joseph Bates was one of the first to practice health reform.

Mr. Lawrence looked at her reproachfully. "I do pray for her," he said, "every minute I live."

"But I mean, can't the elders pray for her, as the Apostle James directs?"

"If there were only godly men of experience living near here," said Mr. Lawrence. "But you know we are few. She prayed in a whisper herself all last night, for the Lord to send someone."

And as he spoke, there was the sound of wheels on the road outside, and a buggy with two men in it drove up and stopped.

They all went to the door, and the two men, having hitched their horse, came up the walk.

"Brother Haskell, of Norfolk!" joyfully exclaimed Mr. Lawrence, holding out his hand.

"Yes, it's Brother Haskell," responded the big, white-bearded man. "I and my brother here have felt impressed by the Lord to drive over these thirty miles to see you. I left my [233] wheat standing ready to be harvested, and the neighbors said I was crazy. And now there must be something needed."

"Indeed there is," answered Mr. Lawrence. "The Lord sent you in answer to prayer. My wife is very low. Will you come in and pray for her?"

They went into the sickroom, but Mrs. Lawrence lay still and deathlike; she could not hear them. They knelt, and first they prayed God to give her strength to hear the prayer. And as [234] they prayed, a faint color came to her cheeks, her eyes became bright, and she spoke to them.

The two men came up the walk.

God had answered. Then they prayed again, fervently, that God would raise her up to health. And rising, Brother Haskell took the sacred oil and poured a little upon her forehead; then laying his hand on her head, he said, "Sister Lawrence, the Lord our God has heard. You shall recover."

And in a moment her strength began to come back to her. She ate food, and in a few days she was able to be up again. Oh, what a happy family when the dear mother was able to be with them again! And what a happy people were they who knew and loved Sister Lawrence as a mother in Israel! And how the neighbors wondered, saying, "What doctor could do that?"

Not long after, there came to them the news that the Spirit of prophecy had spoken in regard to how we should live.

"Horace," said Mrs. Lawrence, "the Lord raised me up from death, and I am going to obey that message in regard to dress. I shall have to make over most of my clothes, but I shall see that I am dressed equally warm all over, in winter. And as for those ridiculous hoops, I am thankful the Lord has spoken against them, for I think they are shameful." [235]

And again, one morning at the breakfast table, a very few weeks later, they were discussing some new directions about health.

"I am glad," said Mr. Lawrence, "for the cleaning up that has come among our people. Strong drink, even cider, never belonged among us; and now tobacco has gone, and tea and coffee. And we are not merely dropping off things; we are putting better food in their place. But I don't know whether we can get any graham flour or not."

"What is this 'graham' flour?" asked his wife.

"Why, Maria, it's just about the same as we used to grind at the water mill, as nearly as I can make out," he answered, "only this man Graham has got his name attached to it. But you see it isn't popular, for the white flour is what folks eat now, and they think it's a sign of wealth. But if I can't buy it, I can get it ground, I suppose, and keep it unbolted, with the bran in. The fine flour has a great deal of the goodness bolted out."

"And pork, father," put in their daughter Ellen. "What are we going to do with our fat hogs, since the Bible says pork isn't fit to eat? Of course, that will not trouble you," she added, for he never ate meat, as the rest of them did. [236]

"We'll have to come up on father's ground, Ellen," said her mother. "As to the hogs, we will certainly not eat them."

"No," said Mr. Lawrence, "and when you come to think of it, it does seem a great waste to put corn into a hog so as to eat it by-and-by. It's better to take it at first hand." [237]

Pioneer Stories

"It does seem a great waste to put corn into a hog." said Mr. Lawrence.

Again, a year or so later, there came the message to their home that a health institute, what we now call a sanitarium, should be built up, a place where the principles of right living could be taught, and where the sick could be cared for by water treatments, and be made well.

"Now that's the right move," declared Mrs. Lawrence. "I've proved the treatments as well as I could give them, you know I have, Horace, and they have helped more than once, when the neighbors' children were sick. And we have better health because of living in the new way.

And it's surely the right thing to establish a health institute, where the sick can get well, and be taught the truth at the same time."

"Yes, it is," he assented, "and we'll have to help what we can to build it up. You see they call for our people to give money for buying a place there in Battle Creek. Yes, yes, Maria, we'll have to help."

"They call for our people to give money to buy a place there in Battle Creek,"—the beginning of the Battle Creek Sanitarium.

And from these little beginnings, all through the ranks the work spread, until ministers and people were very largely practicing and teaching the truth of health reform. Some,—too bad to say it,— did not care enough for it to pay much heed. And it is sad to have to say that many, many, now when the knowledge of how to live healthfully is so much greater than then, seem [238] to care very little for it in their lives. But this is sure, that those who go through to the end will, by being careful how they live, keep their bodies [239] fit for the greatest service of God, so that their health may praise God and make them more able to work for Him.

Today we have many great sanitariums, besides treatment rooms and health restaurants in many cities, and there are many visiting nurses and other health workers all over the land. Still, our great buildings and the great work being done by some are not what count. What counts is whether you and I each make our bodies living temples, holy for the indwelling of God. That is the meaning and the use of health reform. [240]

XXIII

CAMP MEETING

How many times have you been to camp meeting? We have had them now for over seventy years. You remember what I told you of the camp meetings they had before 1844. And you know our camp meetings today are a great deal different from them. We have the big tents for the meetings, instead of holding them out-of-doors, and there are neat rows of family tents lining the camp streets. At night the camp is lighted by electricity. But the camp meetings did not begin with such comforts. Would you like to hear of the first camp meeting held among Seventh-day Adventists?

It was in the year 1868, and the camp was pitched in a "sugar bush"—a maple grove—in the township of Wright, Michigan. There were two large tents, though we might not think them large now. One held the baggage and straw of the campers; the other was used for meetings in stormy weather, and for other special meetings.

The place for the general meeting was in a central spot in the "bush." There was a platform built up for the ministers, and seats for the [241] people were of rough boards. The family tents were pitched in a circle around the central meeting-place. They were made, not of heavy canvas, such as we have now, but of sheeting or drilling. There was just one tent like what we use now, and it had been shipped in from New York. One night there was a heavy thundershower. Did you ever try to keep dry under a sheet out in the rain? That's what those campers had to try. Right away the tents began to leak. There was no getting out of the wet and into a dry corner; they just had to take their wet-

The first Seventh-day Adventist camp meeting was in a maple grove at Wright Michigan.

ting. When morning came and the sun shone out bright, the stamps and fences were covered with bedding and clothing to dry. But when the people looked into the all-canvas tent which had been brought from New York, they saw that there was dry ground; that tent had not leaked, and its people had kept dry.

"Next year," said one, "I'll have a canvas tent too."

"And so will I," said another.

That was the lesson that brought the canvas tents into use.

It was a beautiful grove where they were encamped, and especially so at night. Look up through the [243] dark treetops into the deep black-blue. See the stars shining down through the little holes in the leafy roof. Farther away it makes them seem, somehow. And those faraway little lights are suns, some of them, as big as our sun, or bigger, and though they give but little light to us down here, there are around them great worlds like ours on which they shine more brightly than our sun. And God is beyond them, the great God who made them all, and who calls all by name.

But the stars were not the only light they had for the camp. They had no electric lights, as we have now, but they made some lights that did very well. Driving four stakes into the ground, close together, they built a shallow box on top and filled it with earth. On this they built fires that, blazing high, cheerfully scattered the darkness and gave light a long way. Half a dozen of these fires around the central meeting-place were enough to light the camp.

Outside the camp, too, were great log fires burning; for these September nights were cool. And to these fires came the chilly people to get warm enough to go back and hear the sermon.

After the evening meeting was over, and all had gone to their tents to sleep, around the whole encampment there walked a tall, brown-bearded, spectacled man, and before each tent he would stop and ask in his pleasant voice, "Are you all [244] comfortable for the night?" And if any one wanted anything, the tall man was sure to see he got it. He was one of the principal speakers at the meeting, with Mr. and Mrs. White, but he found time, too, to look after the comfort of everyone. His name was John N. Andrews.

There were only seventeen of the smaller tents, but some of these were divided so as to accommodate a whole church, in the following way. Two-foot

He would ask, "Are you all comfortable for the night?"

boards were placed upright the long way of the tent, so as to leave an aisle in the middle. Between each board and the wall of [245] the tent the space was filled with straw. Each side was then curtained off, and on one side the women slept, and on the other side the men. The poles in the center aisle also supported a board, which by means of pegs in the poles was placed low enough for a table at mealtime and high enough to make a shelf out of the way the rest of the time. Besides those who lived in these tents, many had rooms in near-by houses, and some slept in their wagons. So there were several hundred present.

There was the greatest order at this first camp meeting. After a certain hour no talking was allowed, so that all might sleep. That is something we all need to remember at camp meetings now. And God blessed them. While camp meetings of other people before this time had often been disorderly and had a bad influence, this one was very quiet and well conducted. Many, both of older ones and of children, were brought to Jesus; men who had had trouble with each other were brought together in love; and Christian ties were made stronger.

Everyone who came and listened to the stirring truths from God's servants, and joined with one another in telling of their experiences in the message, declared it was so good a time and so helpful a gathering that they must have another [246] the next year. And they did have, and the next year, and the next, and right along. And our other conferences took it up, so that now camp meetings are held nearly everywhere.

Most of us have a good chance to attend camp meeting, and can have a blessed time if we go to find the Lord; for we shall always find Him there, if we seek Him with true hearts. And it is right, too, to rejoice in meeting our friends whom perhaps we cannot see at any other time. I remember that some of my best friends were made at camp meeting. Were yours?

And the camp meeting may remind us, especially if we go by horse or automobile, of the times we shall have in the new earth, going through the country every Sabbath day and once a month besides, up to the great meeting-place at the New Jerusalem.

Where is your next camp meeting to be held? [247]

XXIV

THE FIRST FOREIGN MISSION

A poor, ragged beggar was passing from door to door in the city of Basle, Switzerland. Something to eat, something to eat, a few centimes to go for a pair of shoes, this was all he seemed to be thinking about; and many a respectable housewife turned him away from her door. What was a beggar—faugh!—to bother about? Besides, it was Saturday, and baking-day; tomorrow was Sunday, and any good Christian woman would be working with might and main to have things in order. Of course, now, if one were a Jew, he might have time on this Saturday to listen to a beggar's whine; and yet that would not be likely for a Jew.

The beggar began even to wish that he might meet a Jew. He stopped before a humble house on a side street, went up the steps, and knocked. The lady who opened the door said kindly, "Come in," and the beggar stepped inside. There in a circle sat a company of people about a tall, brown-bearded, spectacled man, all of them with Bibles in their hands. The beggar almost forgot his need of a few centimes for a pair of [248] shoes. Surely he had found a family of Jews; for was not this a Saturday? And were they not studying the Bible?

Whether he asked for something to eat, really I do not know. I suspect he was actually not very hungry, nor so very much in need of a few centimes. At any rate, he had gained an interest outside his profession; for we see him seated, listening to the reading and talking of these people with Bibles. He hears them studying about the soon coming of Christ. "Surely," says he to

The First Foreign Mission

himself, "these are not Jews. But why are they studying on Saturday? Perhaps they are monks, who do nothing every day but read the Bible. No, no; monks are much more given to eating and drinking or playing dice than to reading the Bible together."

The beggar's mind traveled back over his tramps, back along the Rhine, through Strasburg, Heidelburg, Mainz, Dusseldorf, Elberfeld, —yes, yes, at Elberfeld there were a people who were not Jews who kept Sabbath just like the Jews.

When the Sabbath-school lesson was finished, the beggar began to ask questions. Then they were not Jews, but Christians? Yes. But they kept the seventh day? Yes; for that was what God commands all Christians to do. [249]

"Well," said he, "I never saw anybody like you but once before, and I'm a great traveler. I have been all over Baden and Hesse and Prussia, and even up to Hamburg."

"Did you say you have found other people in Germany who are Christians and who keep the seventh day?" asked Mr. Andrews.

"Yes, once," answered the beggar, "up in Elberfeld. They are kind people. There are not very many of them. I don't know how many. But yes, it's at Elberfeld."

"Do you know any of their names?"

"Why, no. They have a pastor. I meet so many people, though. Let me see—Lundser— Linder—Lindermann—seems that may be his name. I was in his house once. It was on a Saturday, and he had just come from church. He is a kind man. Yes, it's at Elberfeld."

The man seemed very ready to talk, but he could tell nothing more about the company of Sabbath-keepers at Elberfeld. He would not stay to dinner; the mention of it reminded him of his business. "Ah, no, kind people. If only you would give the poor man a bit of bread and something to go with it, and a pfennig—ah, a centime or two, for the shoes that will wear out. Yes, I am going on to Geneva, or it may be Zurich or Freiburg. I fear the Alps, the great [251] mountains. Ah, thank you, madam." And he was gone.

The little Sabbath-keeping company whom we see at Basle on this morning of the beggar's call, was composed of John N. Andrews and his family,

A poor, ragged beggar called for something to eat.

The First Foreign Mission

with a few Swiss believers. And a few years before, M. B. Czechowski, a Polish minister who had met our people in America, had come through this country and preached the Sabbath. A few believed; and happening to find a copy of *The Review and Herald*, they learned of Seventh-day Adventists in America, and sent over two of their men to learn more of the truth. When the second of these, Ademar Vuilleumier, went back to his home in 1874, Mr. Andrews went with him. Thus John N. Andrews was the first foreign missionary we ever sent out.

He believed what the beggar had told them that Sabbath morning; for he knew that God was working with people whom we had not yet reached, and he thought it not impossible that the Sabbath truth had come to some of them.

So, early in the next year, he and J. Erzenberger went down the Rhine River into Prussia, to the city of Elberfeld; and there they found, indeed, a company of Sabbath-keepers, with their pastor, J. H. Lindermann. This minister, five years before, had begun to observe the [252] Sabbath, just from his own study of the Bible. And he taught it to his people, so that about forty of

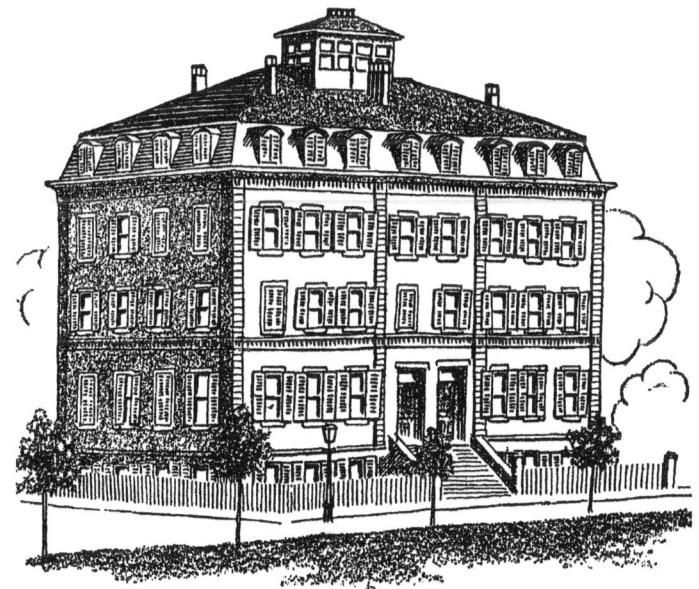

"Imprimerie Polyglotte," our first publishing house in Basle, Switzerland.

them began with him to obey. They did not know any other Christians in the world who kept the Sabbath. When Mr. Andrews and Mr. Erzenberger came down to see them, and told them of Seventh-day Adventists in America, can you imagine how happy they were? Mr. Erzenberger stayed here for about a year, teaching the faith. Not all of these people, however, were willing to accept the whole message, but some [253] were baptized, and they made the first Seventh-day Adventist church in Germany.

Since then the work has spread over all Europe. And whether in peace or in war, the message of Jesus' coming, and of the glad release from sin and its sorrows which that coming will bring, has reached farther and deeper into every corner of the land. [254]

The First Foreign Mission

XXV

SELLING THE BOOKS

The ministers were gathered on the camp ground at Battle Creek for the General Conference of 1880. They had had many matters to talk about and many parts of the work to lay plans for; but they did not know when they came that there was to be presented to them a plan which would grow to be one of the greatest means of spreading the knowledge of the message.

As they stood about talking before the meeting, there came up first to one group and then another and another, a young minister, George A. King. He had two books under his arm, and he would ask two or three ministers to come to the table with him, when he would open these books before them and show them how they could be sold. They were small cloth-covered books, without pictures. One of them was "Thoughts on Daniel," and the other, "Thoughts on the Revelation," both of them written by Uriah Smith. So far they had been published separately, and like all the other literature we had printed, they had very little illustration. [255]

But George King, who had been selling books on health for several years, and before that such tracts and pamphlets as we had, believed that the larger books, if illustrated and made attractive, could be sold by the thousands. Of course, some of the ministers in their tent meetings and some of the people through their neighborhoods had given away a good deal of literature and had sold some, but they did not get much, if anything, for selling them, and so could not make a living at it, or give all their time to it. Even George King, when he first became a Seventh-day Adventist, and had gone out to sell tracts, had had to

Selling the Books

stop in the fall and work in the fields or woods to make enough money to buy his clothing.

Now, he told the ministers, it was possible to make books which the colporteur could sell for enough to give him something to live on. He called attention to what Mrs. White had written about the great importance of selling our publications, and he suggested that books be properly prepared, and that hundreds of men and women engage in selling them. He proposed that the Review and Herald publishing house now put the two books into one, and make the book,

"Thoughts on Daniel and the Revelation," with large pictures and good bindings, and put [256] on it a price which would permit the colporteur to take half the money for selling it.

The ministers at this General Conference were glad to hear this suggestion from Mr. King, and to hear his assurance, from his own experience and faith, that these books could be sold. The Review and Herald agreed to illustrate the book and to print five thousand if Mr. King would take the first thousand. This he did; and so the first large subscription book that was printed was "Thoughts on Daniel and the Revelation." This first edition was soon sold and others were quickly printed.

After this Mr. King not only canvassed, but spent a great deal of time in getting others to canvass and in training them. For several years thereafter, while he sold books in the winter, he went to the various camp meetings in summertime, and taught new colporteurs how to handle the books. In a short time there were hundreds at work, not only with "Daniel and the Revelation," but with other books which were soon illustrated and printed, like "The Great Controversy between Christ and Satan," "Patriarchs and Prophets," and "Bible Readings."

This was the beginning of the colporteur work among us, which has so greatly helped in extending the publishing work as the years have [258] gone by. Where we then had two publishing houses, we now have eighty-three, which print the gospel in over two hundred languages. In place of the one subscription book and the few tracts, pamphlets, and small books, there are 2,338 different books, 1,355 pamphlets, and 5,234 tracts. And instead of the one man,

He would open these books before them, and show them how they could be sold.

George King, who stepped out with faith and courage to sell our books and live by doing it, there are now more than 3,000 men and women all over the world who are giving all their time to the scattering of the truth-filled pages "like the leaves of autumn." [259]

XXVI

VISITING AN AFRICAN CHIEF

Kalaka was a great man among the Suto people. He was not a chief, but he knew two languages, the French and the English, besides his own and several other dialects. He had been educated to translate the Bible, and he taught his people much of the true God.

One day, in the year 1889, there came to his hut in Basutoland, Africa, a missionary who had come from faraway America to talk with his people. Kalaka knew this from a letter the missionary carried from some Suto people whom the missionary had met. "We are very anxious," they said, "that Pastor Stephen N. Haskell, who carries this letter, should talk to you about God and His word. He knows God, and he can tell you much."

Kalaka was glad to see Mr. Haskell, and after talking with him awhile, he said, "I will take you to the high chief, and have you talk with him." Mr. Haskell had a letter to this man, who was called the Paramount Chief, as he was chief over all the chiefs of Basutoland. Whenever anything had to be decided about their country [260] or their people, they would come together in a council, and make up their minds together about it. Sometimes they didn't agree, and sometimes they all agreed against the Paramount Chief. This troubled the old chief. He thought they all ought to see alike, and to be alike.

When Mr. Haskell came and talked with him, the Paramount Chief told him how bad it was that his council would not agree with him. Mr. Haskell could not understand the Suto language, but Kalaka interpreted for him. That

When the cheif told his troubles, Mr. Haskell pointed to a tree.

Pioneer Stories

is, Mr. Haskell would say something in English, then Kalaka would tell it to the chief in Suto; then the chief would say something in Suto, and Kalaka would tell it to Mr. Haskell in English.

When the chief told his troubles, Mr. Haskell pointed to a tree under which they were sitting, and said, "Look! Look at that tree, and tell me how many branches on it are just alike."

The chief looked. "Why," he said, "there are no two alike."

"And yet they are all good," said Mr. Haskell, "and the tree needs them all to make leaves for shade, and fruit for eating. If they all were just alike, the same size and shape, and growing in the same direction, they would not be nearly so useful, nor the tree so beautiful. If the fruit is good, you do not care what is the shape of [261] the branch. That is like your council of chiefs. If they were all alike it would be very bad. You could not do much, nor so well."

"Yes, yes," cried the chief, "I see. That is very true, Pastor Haskell."

The old chief was delighted with this illustration, which explained to him how men can be different and yet be doing the same work. And he remembered it well for many years, as you shall see.

Kalaka also was much struck with Haskell's illustration, and with his talks. After this he traveled for six weeks with him through the country to find different tribes whom Mr. Haskell wanted to visit. Driving along in their covered wagon, they read the Bible together. Mr. Haskell did not tell him anything of the faith he held, but when they would read the verses that taught such truths, he would just emphasize the words. And Kalaka saw and believed. Still he would not say so. Thus they read about the Sabbath, and the coming of Jesus, and baptizing. They read the story in Acts 8 of Philip's baptizing the eunuch, where it says *they went down into the water*. Kalaka belonged to a society that believed in sprinkling, not in immersion. But here it says the eunuch went into the water to be baptized. Kalaka did not say [263] anything about it, however, and Mr. Haskell did not ask him. But one day as they were driving along on their way toward home, they stopped by the side of a stream to let their horses graze. Kalaka and Mr. Haskell sat down on the grass by the stream. Suddenly Kalaka spoke up. "'See, here is water,' he said; 'what doth hinder me to be baptized?'"

Visiting an African Chief

"See,' he said. here is water. 'What doth hinder me to be baptized?'"

And in the words of Philip, Mr. Haskell replied, "'If thou believest with all thine heart, thou mayest.'"

And Kalaka at once replied, " I believe that Jesus Christ is the Son of God."

He decided to keep the Sabbath, and accepted all the faith, and was baptized. Afterwards he translated Mrs. White's book, "Steps to Christ," into his language, and thus the way was prepared for the message to go to the Suto people.

Nine years afterwards J. M. Freeman was sent to Africa to work for these people. When he came into Basutoland he went to the chiefs to get some land on which to build a mission. But the chiefs had all been instructed by the French not to let him have any, and they said no, he could not stay. But the old chief asked him some questions, and soon found out that he believed what Pastor Haskell believed.

"Are you of the same religion," he asked Mr. Freeman, "as that missionary who came here [265] some years ago, and talked to me about the trees?"

"Yes," answered Mr. Freeman, "I am." For he knew the story of Mr. Haskell's illustration.

Pioneer Stories

"Then you can have any piece of land in my country you want," said the old chief. So the Basuto Mission was established, and it has been there and has done a good work ever since. [266]

In Basutoland.

XXVII

THE PITCAIRN

The Sabbath schools could do it! And the Sabbath schools did it. There was a ship to be built, a missionary ship; and where could the money come from to build it? Some thought the General Conference could give it. But the General Conference had not enough money for its regular work. And some thought that if men went out and begged the people to give it, at least a large part of the needed sum could be gotten. But it was said that *might* do, and it *might* cost almost as much to send the men out as all the money that would be gathered.

Well, here are the Sabbath schools, said they at last, already organized, already giving money; let's get the Sabbath School Association to give a year's collections for the building of the ship, and then through our papers let's urge the Sabbath schools to give more than they have been giving, and make up the twelve thousand dollars we need. And so they did.

You see this was away back in 1890, when our Sabbath schools were not so many as now, and twelve thousand dollars was a big sum for them [267] to raise. But they went to work; and the boys and the girls brought their pennies and their nickels and their dimes, and once or twice I heard of a dollar given by a girl or a boy. They made their money by running errands, by hoeing corn and picking potato bugs, by making and selling pincushions, and in a hundred other ways. And how glad they were to bring in those hard-earned pennies and nickels and dimes! Of course the older people gave their money, too. And all together, they did it. The Sabbath schools did it. And the ship was started building in the shipyards of Vallejo, California.

Pioneer Stories

What was the ship for? Well, I will tell you. Away down in the South Pacific Ocean lies a lonely island, only two miles long and three fourths of a mile wide, a high, rocky point pushed up above old ocean's surface. Though so small and so craggy, it is covered with trees and other plants, and it is the home of thousands upon thousands of sea birds, while wild goats live on the rocky steeps. And there also, in the midst of their orange groves and banana plantations and yam patches, live a little company of gentle folk.

So the ship Pitcairn was built.

Over a hundred years ago their forefathers came there to live, where none were living before. But these their forefathers were not gentle, but very fierce and rough. They were English sailors who had mutinied on the good ship "Bounty," and cast their captain, with a few men, adrift on the wide ocean in an open boat. Then they brought the "Bounty" to Pitcairn Island, with ten native women and six men whom they had persuaded to come with them from the island of Tahiti.

But they were all quarrelsome and wicked, and it was not many years before they had killed one another off, until only two white men remained, with several native women and about thirty children. These two white men were named John Adams and Edward Young. When they alone were left, these men began to feel very sorry for their wicked ways (though they [269] had been the best of all the men), and very sorry for the poor children who were growing

The Pitcairn

up without knowing anything of God or rightdoing. And they repented, and prayed to God for forgiveness, and set about to teach the children.

But very soon Edward Young died, and this left John Adams all alone. He kept hard at work teaching his children and the children of his dead companions; and very soon the place which had been so foul with blood and wickedness, came to be a place of beautiful order and love. Just one Bible they had, which John Adams had saved; but as they learned the word of God, passage after passage, very soon they had much of the Bible in their minds. And as they learned to read and write, they copied many parts for themselves.

It was a lonely place, though they were happy. Never once in thirty years did they see a ship, or any other faces than their own. But at last a vessel stopped there and found them; and when it went back to old England, its captain told the world about the settlement on Pitcairn Island, and how out of the mutinous gang of the "Bounty" there had come a Christian community of peace and quietness.

In 1876 James White and John Loughborough, hearing of this island, sent a package of papers and tracts to the people, but they did not [270] know whether they would reach them or not, for very seldom did a ship pass by Pitcairn Island. They did reach them, however, and this was the first that Pitcairn heard of Seventh-day Adventists. The people read the papers, and for awhile they almost decided to keep the Sabbath; but since there was no one to teach them further, they dropped the matter at last.

Ten years afterwards John I. Tay determined that he would go to Pitcairn and carry the message to the islanders. He landed there one day in October, 1886, and stayed about six weeks. By this time the people all had Bibles, and Mr. Tay studied with them, from the Bible, the truths of the coming of the Lord, the Sabbath, and all the [271] rest. And before he left, every one, man, woman, and child, was keeping the Sabbath and looking for Jesus to come.

John Tay went to other islands in the Pacific Ocean to carry the message. But he found it so hard to get to many of them, where ships did not call very often, that he came home to America, to ask for a ship of our own. At first the brethren did not think of building one. Instead they sent A. J. Cudney in a small ship which they bought and named the "Phoebe Chapman." With a

There in the midst of their orange groves live a company of gentle folk.

missionary crew of five men, Cudney started out in this ship to go to Pitcairn. Mr. Tay had gone down to Tahiti to wait for Mr. Cudney to pick him up, when they would go together to Pitcairn, and afterwards to other islands.

The "Phoebe Chapman" sailed from Honolulu, in the Hawaiian Islands, July 31, 1888, and should have reached Tahiti in a few weeks. But nothing more was ever heard from her or the people in her. No doubt they perished in some great storm. God knew His reasons, though we do not, why Mr. Cudney and his brother missionaries should not reach their field of labor. He laid them away to rest in the bosom of the old ocean, until that day when the sea shall give up her dead to receive their reward. And were they not martyrs for Jesus, as much as any who have [272] died for Him, though they perished not under the spears or the axes of savage men, nor languished in dungeons and chains, but gave up their lives to the storm-king of the waters?

When John Tay saw that it was of no more use to wait for the "Phoebe Chapman," he came back to America and urged that a boat be built. And this was the time when the Sabbath schools were set to work to get the money for its building. Five months it was in building, and then, launched on the blue waters of San Francisco Bay, it lay ready for its mission to the islands of the sea. It was named the "Pitcairn." E. H. Gates and his wife, A. J. Read and his wife, and John I. Tay and his wife went with the ship. Captain Marsh was over the crew.

The Pitcairn

First they steered for Pitcairn Island. After sailing many, many weary days, on the morning of November 25, 1890, they saw the high peaks of Pitcairn rise over the waters.

The Pitcairn islanders had known that the ship was in building, and were eagerly waiting for it to come. Every morning, for many weeks, the children and young people would race to the brow of the hill above the landing place, or to the higher peaks, to see if the ship was in sight. And on this glad morning they came bounding back to the village, shouting, "Sail ho! The ship's [273] here! The ship's here!" And the strong young men of the island launched their boat and drove through the breakers, and rowed out to where the ship lay hove to. A rope was thrown to them, and they clambered over the ship's side, to greet first, with happy faces and busy tongues, old Brother Tay, and then his fellow missionaries.

That day and the next were holidays to Pitcairn, but holidays filled with glad praise to God for His goodness in sending them teachers.

The "Pitcairn" stayed three weeks by the island; and then went on to other islands. They cruised about the South Seas, leaving papers and books, and teaching the people wherever they went. Mr. Read and his wife were located in Tahiti to teach, while Mr. Tay went to Fiji.

When the year had gone by, the "Pitcairn" sailed back, touching at these places again on its way to America. But two of the good people who had gone out with her were never to come back. Captain Marsh, who had guided the little vessel so safely over the great ocean, and who who had joined with the others in telling the truth, had died, and been buried in the island of New Zealand. And John Tay, who had labored so faithfully to bring about this means of carrying the truth, was taken sick in Fiji. He died, and was laid to rest in that foreign land. But he [275] could count his work done; for he had set others to work, and the message has spread, since then, over all the great island groups of the South Seas.

When the "Pitcairn" came back to San Francisco and reported the work that had been started, all the Adventist people rejoiced. And don't you think we boys and girls who had helped the good missionary ship were happy to think what our money had done?

"Sail ho! The ship's here! The Ship's here!"

The Pitcairn

The "Pitcairn" went back and forth, year after year, making four voyages in all, and spreading the truth far and wide. But by the last of these voyages, so many more ships had been built for trade and travel in the Pacific Ocean, and it was so much easier to send missionaries and books wherever we needed to, that it was thought we need not keep up the expense of a separate ship. So at last the ship "Pitcairn" was sold. But the work that was begun through it has never stopped, and it never will stop until all is finished, and from the islands of the sea shall many come to greet the great King in His glory. [276]

XXVIII

WHAT YOU WERE BORN FOR

Dear boys and girls, in this book I have told you many stories of the men and women who began and carried on the message of the second advent of our Lord Jesus Christ. It is now more than a hundred years since that message began, and you do not need to be told (though in some cases I have told you) that those who first studied and preached the message are now sleeping in Jesus, waiting for the great day when He shall call them forth again to eternal life. You may also know that nearly all the pioneers of the Seventh-day Adventists have died, though at the point to which I have brought these stories, about 1890, most of them were living.

These are the *pioneer* stories of the second advent message; that is, the stories of the men and women who ventured out in the forefront and showed the way to those who should come after. And there have been thousands who have come after. The half century since these stories end has been filled with marvelous manifestations of God's providence and guidance in the carrying of His great message. Where there was [277] one messenger then, there are a thousand now. Where the message was being given in one language then, it is being given in hundreds of languages now. Amidst the shock of warring peoples, of crumbling kingdoms, of distress of nations, the glorious cause of the second advent message is going to the farthest corners of the earth. Many books have been written which contain parts of the record of these heroic missionary labors, and in them you will find the stories that carry on to our present times.

Jesus says, *"Even before you were born, I chose you and set you your work."*

Pioneer Stories

But now, while you have been reading or hearing about all these faithful men and women whom God called into His service, I wonder if you have thought what you have to do with it all. When you read of how God called William Miller to His great work, and how He strengthened the young and frail Ellen Harmon to carry His word, do you think that you just happened to hear of this great advent message; or do you think God planned for you to fill the places of those whom He has laid to rest?

You are successors to those earliest heralds, Miller, Irving, and Wolff.

Away back in the days of Israel's kings there was a boy whom the Lord called to be His prophet. But young Jeremiah shrank from the great work. He said, "O Lord, I cannot speak; for I am only a child." But the Lord said to him, "Do not say, 'I am a child and do not know what [279] I should do'; for I will send you wherever you should go, and I tell you whatever you should say. Do not be afraid, for I will be with you and always deliver you." And so it was throughout Jeremiah's life. He suffered much. He was imprisoned, and

What You Were Born For

starved, and threatened with death, but God always cared for him, and he was always faithful, though he began as only a child to do God's bidding. More than that, God said to him, "Even before you were born I [280] chose you, and set you your work as a prophet." I think that was a wonderful honor, don't you, to be chosen for the work before he was born? And yet, you know, I believe that God chooses every one in the same way. For the Bible says, in the fourth chapter of Ephesians, that God chose every one of us in Jesus before the foundation of the world. And just as surely as He chose you, He chose you to do some special work for Him. And that is what you were born for.

You are heirs of those pioneers, James White, Ellen G White, and Joseph Bates.

If you ask [281] me what is the exact work you were born to do, I cannot tell you. But if you ask God, He can tell you, for He knows. And He will tell you. It may not ever be that He will talk to you with His voice, as He did to Samuel, and as He did, perhaps, to Jeremiah. But if He does not, He will tell you by impressing your mind as you read the Bible, by the opportunities He gives you for education, by the way He shapes the circumstances of your life, and by the talents of mind and body He gives you.

It may be that you are to be a doctor or a nurse, healing the sick while you

Pioneer Stories

teach them the [282] way of life, as Jesus did. If you have a desire to become a Christian physician or nurse, and show it by helping all you can now, I think that is pretty good evidence that God wants you to do such work for Him. And when you have chances to learn how to treat the sick or how to give first aid in accidents, or how to keep your health by right habits of eating and exercise and dress and all the other laws, I am sure you will be eager to take and use such opportunities. And anyway, whether or not we become nurses and doctors, every one

You are chosen to bear the standard carried by such men as Smith, Andrews, and Loughborough.

of us should know and do all we can to keep well and to make the sick well.

It may be that you are to be a teacher, whether in the schoolroom or outside, and by your teaching you are to help others to know more of the wisdom and love of God, as Jesus did. If this is so, I am sure that you will be eager not only to read a great deal of history and science and religion, but to *do* all that you learn. For I want to tell you a secret, and it is this: No one can be really a teacher who does not do things he teaches. If he simply reads them or hears them, and then tells them over, he is a teller, not a teacher. Jesus never taught anything He had not first experienced, and if we are to be like Him, the Great Teacher, we should do as He did. The teacher must be able to do [283] things

You must finish the work nobly carried on by such devoted workers as Kilgore, Haskell, and Butler.

with his hands as well as with his brain. Whether it is in agriculture, or mechanics, or cooking and housekeeping, or some other kind of work, the one who can do things, and not merely tell things, is able to be the true teacher. And then, of course, he loves to help people; for teaching is really just helping people who need help, [284] whether it is in books or in everyday practical things.

It may be that you are to be an evangelist, and that you will preach the gospel to the poor and needy, as Jesus did. And you may think you would have to grow up before you could be an evangelist; but that is not so. For let me tell you again, the man who can only tell things, and cannot do things, cannot be really an evangelist. Jesus was able to preach the gospel because all His life He had helped people. When He was a boy, He did errands for His mother and His brothers and sisters, and He visited the sick and sorrowful, and He often fed the hungry, even if He had to go without His own dinner to do it. I am sure that He never kicked the cow, or forgot to water the horses, and that if He saw a starved cat, or a lamb with a broken leg, He cared for it. And it was because He acted out the love of God all through His life, that He was able to preach the love of God in such a way as made men believe Him and follow Him into the kingdom. So you can start being an evangelist right now.

And now a last thing let me tell you, children: There are not too many people to fill the places God has waiting. This day, while I write, I am thinking of a good many places, over in Spain, [285] and down in Brazil, and far back in China, and deep in Africa, and down in the South Sea islands, as well as right here in America, where there are calls for missionaries, and we can't find enough evangelists and doctors and teachers and canvassers and editors and secretaries and printers and trained farmers and mechanics to fill them. It will always be so to the end; God's work is so great that every single one who will give himself to the Lord and be willing to be trained for the work will find a place where he can work and grow. And this is what you were born for. [286]

We invite you to view the complete
selection of titles we publish at:

www.TEACHServices.com

Scan with your mobile
device to go directly
to our website.

or write or email us your praises, reactions,
or thoughts about this or any other book we publish at:

TEACH Services, Inc.
P U B L I S H I N G

www.TEACHServices.com

P.O. Box 954
Ringgold, GA 30736

info@TEACHServices.com

TEACH Services, Inc., titles may be purchased in bulk for educational, business, fund-raising, or sales promotional use. For information, please e-mail:

BulkSales@TEACHServices.com

Finally, if you are interested in seeing
your own book in print, please contact us at

publishing@TEACHServices.com

We would be happy to review your manuscript for free.

www.ingramcontent.com/pod-product-compliance
Lightning Source LLC
Chambersburg PA
CBHW070536170426
43200CB00011B/2446